Egos & Eggshells

Managing For Success In Today's Workplace

MARGOT ROBINSON, M.A.

Stanton & Harper Books

P.O. Box 21585
Greensboro, NC 27420

Note from the Author

Times have changed and so has the word "supervisor." In the past, the word was applied to someone who was a front line manager.

Throughout this book, I have used the word to mean someone who develops people. My definition would include a coach on a basketball team who enables team members to be their best. Although the word supervisor can still be applied to the people on the front line, it also describes those who empower their employees at all different levels of an organization.

At work we are either supervised or we supervise. It is for the second group, those who supervise, that I write.

So who should read this book? Anyone who supervises people. That includes all management, church personnel, sports clubs, volunteers and government workers. **EGOS & EGGSHELLS** was written to make these people more successful in their work.

Remember, your people are your most valuable resource. Without them, you have nothing. I urge you and your organization to use these proven methods as you turn the corner towards the 21st century.

Acknowledgments

It has been exciting to have friends and business associates out there rooting for me during this project. This is a time I would like to thank them for all their support.

My husband, Stephen Planson, has been the backbone of this book. Without his love, support and being by my side, this book would not have been written.

My parents, Bill and Virginia Robinson, have always been there with their love and encouragement. It has made me the person I am today.

Janet Fox, a friend, a journalist and a mentor, has been there for me since the day I started my business. It has been an honor and a joy to work with someone so talented.

Sherry Poole has been the most delightful graphic artist to be with. She has the ability to take a mess and turn it into a beautiful creation. What talent!

April Hutchinson, Kathy Lubbers and Miles Peterson have been my brainstorming group. Wow! What energy, what insight, and what a fantastic bunch of people to get creative with.

Mary Alice Watkins' enthusiasm helped me through the research stage. As a reference librarian, she is the best!

●

In memory of my grandmother,
Kathryn Ball Matson
she will always ride with me in my heart.

●

More Praise for Egos & Eggshells

"Egos & Eggshells engages and challenges you as a leader and manager. In this fast paced and ever changing business environment, Margot Robinson provides a tool kit of knowledge which facilitates in the blending of leadership style, human resources management and strategic business thinking."

Ruth Wisniewski, Senior Trainer, RJR Tobacco

"Great reading for new or experienced managers alike! Excellent examples, convenient summaries and self-development steps throughout. I came away with new ideas and suggestions I plan to implement in my department immediately."

Julie A. TeKippe, Vice President
American Television & Communications Corp.

"A book that I would put on my 'gem list.' Margot Robinson has succinctly and clearly articulated principles and strategies for effective leadership. Using clear language (no management jargon here) and examples, the author describes how supervisors can most effectively work in partnership with employees to generate results for the organization."

Ron Cadieux, Ph.D. Manager, Ashland Chemical Company

"Filled with common sense and simple principles to help us 'do the right things' right."

Regina Wright, Manager, Hallmark Cards, Inc.

Contents

Egos & Eggshells
Managing For Success In Today's Workplace

INTRODUCTION · 1

Chapter One · 7
THE NEW SUPERVISOR
Redefining the Role

Chapter Two · 23
ALL THE KING'S MEN
Leading Your Team to Achievement

Chapter Three · 41
THE RESPONSIBLE EGO
Getting Power Through Empowerment

Chapter Four · 55
HAM RADIOS AND SMOKE SIGNALS
Communicating Clearly

Chapter Five · 83
COLONELS AND CAPTAINS
Empowering Your Employees Through Delegation

Chapter Six · 105
HUMPTY DUMPTY: PUTTING ALL THE PIECES TOGETHER AGAIN
Building Teamwork Into Your Team

Chapter Seven · 121
EGGSHELLS ON A ROLE
Motivating Your Team to Achieve Peak Performance

Chapter Eight · 141
ROSES AND THORNS: TELLING IT THE WAY IT IS
Evaluating Employee Performance

Chapter Nine · 165
AS THE HOUR GLASS TRICKLES
Filling Your Time With Meaning

Chapter Ten · 183
KEEPING HUMPTY DUMPTY TOGETHER
Managing the Stress of Supervisory Leadership

INDEX · 204

Introduction

"The credit belongs to the man who is actually in the arena, whose face is actually marred by dust and sweat and blood; who strives valiantly; who errs and comes up short again and again, who knows the great enthusiasms, the great devotions, and spends himself in a worthy cause; who at the least knows the triumph of high achievement; and who, at the worst, if he fails, at least fails while daring greatly, so that his place shall never be with those cold and timid souls who know neither victory nor defeat."

— Theodore Roosevelt

The business arena, especially the area of management, is no place for timid souls. Although the idea of who a supervisor is and in what role supervisors perform for an organization is changing dramatically, they will always fill a unique and often tough role within a company. This book is designed to help all supervisors, regardless of where they are in the work place, to fill that role.

As a supervisor, you probably often feel caught in a squeeze between upper management's demands and subordinate employees' needs. Your boss pressures you to meet company objectives. Your employees demand to be heard. Everyone turns to you to answer their needs.

You walk among tender egos that need stroking, and strong egos that need channeling.

You also tread among eggshells. The Humpty Dumpty of the nursery rhyme was an egg, and the work place is full of Humpty Dumptys — ideas and procedures that have fallen from organizational walls, shattering their shells and littering the road to achievement. You have to decide whether to attempt the delicate task of putting them together again, or to sweep them aside and make way for new approaches.

There are times the strain can make you wonder whether you really **want** this job.

As a supervisor, you might have been thrust into your position with little advance training or support. You've been pushed from your familiar wall, and now you face an unfamiliar routine. You've moved directly from your old job into a new office, with little more than a handshake and a good-luck wish. Your new routine looks like so many eggshell fragments that you have to assemble into a coherent whole without any model to go by. So you go from being a tremendous success on your old job to feeling insecure and unsteady behind a desk. This book will help you feel less insecure.

As a supervisor, you may also face the frustrations of being given tremendous responsibility with very little power. Management expects you to maintain peak performance in your department; yet you sometimes feel as if you've been given little control over many elements affecting production. Maybe you have to run every decision past your superiors. Or you have to cut through several layers of red tape to get necessary equipment and supplies.

Your employees see you as the company personified. To them, you are the boss. They don't think about the fact that you too have bosses. They come to you with their complaints, requests and needs, and expect you to fill them. To them, you are management; you are the company. They hold *you* responsible for giving them answers, granting their requests and representing their interests.

The irony of the situation is that you don't necessarily have the vested power to get results — either for the managers pressing down on you or for the employees expecting you to answer their needs. You are not powerless, however. In this book, I will show you how to develop real power, versus vested power. Vested power accompanies a title. But real power is the ability to *inspire* — rather than *demand* — peak performance in your employees and to motivate them to produce. It results from mutually beneficial relationships with other departments — relationships that will enable you to get results for your team.

If you can achieve real power, you will be one of the most important team members in your company. You will be a primary force behind your business. Enabling you to do just that is my objective for this book.

Supervisors Face a Tougher Job Than Ever

Surviving in a supervisory position has always required guts. You have to have the guts to withstand the pressure from the top and the bottom ends of your business. You also have to hold up under the demands from outside competition and other economic forces. You have to make effective decisions quickly, to know how to read people and to get the best from them, to recognize trends in your industry, to anticipate and facilitate change, and to constantly answer the question: "How can we do what we do more effectively?"

Many people are finding, however, that supervising has never been so complicated or so challenging as it is today. Intense global competition, tight money, downsizing, drastic labor shortages and increasingly sophisticated technology have all compounded the pressures of managing a staff effectively.

For one thing, if you work for one of the many companies forced to thin their middle-management ranks almost into non-existence, you are expected to shoulder more responsibility. You have more work and more pressure, and you also have less management support. There just aren't enough middle-level managers to go around. So you will quite often find yourself on your own.

The same companies that have cut back on managers have also trimmed their production staffs; so top management expects you to get higher productivity from fewer people. In addition to the self-inflicted labor crunch, a shortage of qualified employees has also made your job more difficult in recent years. And analysts are saying that this is a trend of the future — leaner and meaner organizations.

Secondly, advanced and rapidly changing technology has complicated production, therefore complicating your job. You must maintain production through increasingly sophisticated equipment and information systems. Trying to keep up with new developments can seem like a full-time job.

These added pressures are only one side of the lean-corporation coin. Supervisors face uncertain futures. The elimination of jobs has reduced opportunities for advancement within many companies. Time was when a hard-working employee could count on a steady ascent up the corporate ladder. Today, only those who work both hard and smart can expect to move upward.

Opportunity Lurks Within Challenge

No doubt about it, supervising is more demanding than ever. Yet, never has it offered such potential for career achievement and personal growth. The same factors that have cut promotions for managers have also opened up doors.

Leaders on all levels are earning the respect they deserve. Companies have begun to recognize that they are more dependent than ever on all employees who have supervisory duties. Why? So they can maintain their competitive edge in the marketplace. With the added responsibilities you must handle, comes added power and value.

The vacuum created by the elimination of middle management is forcing business leaders to give these employees more control; more room to experiment and innovate. Maintaining the status quo won't cut it in today's business arena. You now have the freedom to make a difference for your company by pursuing ways to improve productivity and performance. The personal satisfaction in such a position is unlimited. The potential for growth is immeasurable.

Professional rewards come as you develop into more than an order-giver. As you become a force behind your company's success, you become a leader, a valuable member of the management team.

Open the Door to Opportunity

Because the demands on supervisors have changed, supervisors also must change. The strategies that produced results 10 years ago won't save you from the dangers pawing the ground in today's business world. Supervisors need to develop their skills and understanding to meet the challenges facing them.

Egos and Eggshells answers that need.

You can step into the arena and rise to meet the challenges facing you on the job — a job that has become increasingly complex — by going beyond coordinating assignments and meeting production quotas. You can be more than an overseer — someone who hands out work orders and cracks a whip. You can become a leader — a person who makes a difference for the company, for your team members and for yourself.

This book gives you the tools to deal skillfully with the egos and stride confidently among the eggshells. It shows you how to meet the challenge. You have to supply the commitment.

1

THE NEW SUPERVISOR
Redefining the Role

"The world stands aside to let anyone pass who knows where he is going." [1]

— David Starr Jordan

As a supervisor, you are the control mechanism that makes the wheels turn. It would be hard to overstate the impact you have on your company's performance.

Top executives may map the course for a company. They may decide on objectives and draw up strategies. You turn the visions of the executive suite into action in the workplace.

The vice president of finance may decree that costs in your department have to be reduced by 50%, but you are the one responsible for cutting out waste and increasing efficiency to make it happen.

The vice president of marketing may engineer a plan that increases sales by 25% in one month, but you and your team have to provide the service.

Supervisors have always been key players in transforming drawing-board sketches into bottom-line results. Yet, in recent years, the position of supervisor has grown to include more responsibility, more freedom and more influence.

Tremendous changes have swept the business world in the past 15 years, causing shifts of power and responsibility throughout organizations in all industries. The demands of today's complex and competitive business environment are forcing companies to redefine the roles of people responsible for getting action at the production level. The definition of a supervisor has changed drastically in the past decade.

As a supervisor today, you play a more active role in your company's fight to maintain an edge in an intensely competitive global marketplace.

Understanding The Factors Reshaping The Role Of Supervisor

Several factors have brought on the change in responsibility and influence for supervisors:

FACTOR #1: *The rapid pace of change*

Change, which bears down on businesses like a runaway locomotive, is such an overwhelming factor in the management of a business today that talking about it has become almost cliché.

Even the dullest business leaders understand that the current rate of change, never before experienced, forces them to reorganize management strategies. They must constantly analyze shifts in market trends, advances in technology, and any other factors influencing the business environment. They must be prepared to respond to changes in their industries or markets instantly or risk being run over by their competitors.

How does this factor affect your role as supervisor? Significantly.

Business leaders know they can't keep track of and respond to every change or development in their fields. They have had to pass along much of this responsibility to other managers.

They understand that businesses can no longer afford to wait for commands to trickle down from top management. Businesses have to respond to new market trends or advances in technology immediately. Waiting to respond to your reports that customer needs are changing takes too much time. You and your team need to take the initiative, to be aware of and responsive to customer needs and industry developments.

For a business to be responsive, it must empower people on all levels, to anticipate and adapt to change as it happens.

As a supervisor in this explosive business environment, you have much more freedom than your predecessors. If you identify a customer need, you can design a plan for responding to that need. If you recognize a way to improve production, management encourages you to implement it. Basically, you have more flexibility for exploring ways in which you can improve what you and your employees do.

Keep in mind, however, that more freedom equals more responsibility. The same people who have given you more control also expect you to keep your finger on the pulse of production. They depend on you to pay attention to events and trends affecting production and quality. That means staying informed on industry developments, keeping an eye on the competition, and tuning in to customer needs. You have to learn to anticipate change and to develop appropriate responses to it. You have to develop ***vision.***

Time was when "vision" was a word heard only in executive suites. Today, the upper management in smart companies is spreading the vision gospel to all its employees. They want people who can see beyond what their teams are accomplishing today. They want you to focus on what you and your employees are capable of achieving.

FACTOR #2: *The financial squeeze*

Skyrocketing business costs, aggravated by the constant battle to beat competitors' prices without sacrificing quality, have put a stranglehold on organizations in every industry. To maintain healthy profit margins without pricing themselves out of the market, businesses have to keep slicing away the fat from their operations.

I'm talking about downsizing, a 1980s trend that left the management of many businesses skinny. If it seems as though there aren't many middle managers around these days, it's because there aren't. Corporate America has eliminated throngs of middle-level managers.

Everywhere I do my workshops, I see more people scared about what is happening. All across America, businesses are realizing that they aren't "fat city" anymore. If you are one of the lucky ones who survived the cutbacks, you are going to fill the gap created by those who left.

With less direction and input from the top, supervisors are making more decisions, taking more control of their departments and accepting more responsibility for production results.

FACTOR #3: *A new work ethic*

Probably one of the biggest changes you have to deal with is the change in the people working for you. Today's employees aren't the same people who filled this country's businesses 20 years ago.

Supervisors have to cope with a new work ethic, which doesn't respond well to iron-handed whip-cracking — once a common management style. Force won't work against this new ethic, strengthened by a serious labor shortage (which analysts predict will worsen as we head into the 21st century). You can't make today's employees work; you have to make them want to work.

What has caused this new work ethic? A number of factors.

For one thing, people today want more than a paycheck. They want satisfaction from their jobs. David Campbell, author of *If I'm in Charge Here, Why Is Everybody Laughing?* said, "Making a living is necessary and often satisfying; eventually, making a difference becomes more important."

Your employees don't want to be treated like machines. They are not robots you can start up in the morning, program to produce all day, then shut down at quitting time. People want more than to be kept busy with tasks. They want to get involved in their work. They want to have a voice, and they want to be heard. They want to use their brains. They want to unleash their creativity and to share ideas.

Secondly, today's workers don't like to be ordered around. They want to be involved in the planning stages of an assignment or project. They want to participate in decisions and designs. They want managers to ask for their opinions.

Third, today's workers demand control over their jobs and over their careers. They want to know that they can control their progress through the quality and quantity of their work. They insist on clearly defined rewards based on performance, not on a system that treats everyone the same regardless of commitment or skill.

Finally, workers today demand respect. They won't tolerate supervisors who treat them like second-class citizens. And, if they don't get respect, they can usually find a job somewhere else.

Today's employees respond to understanding, empathy and involvement, with an increased commitment to production and quality. Keep in mind, however, that this coin has a flip side. Employees will react with hostility and dissension (*even if it's only passive*) to domineering and seemingly insensitive managers.

What Will It Take To Meet These Demands?

Supervising as we have known it in the past won't meet the demands of today's business world. Certainly, the bottom line of supervising has remained basically the same. As a supervisor, you are responsible for accomplishing your company's objectives by directing and coordinating the efforts of your employees.

The philosophies and strategies you use for achieving this objective, however, have changed dramatically.

Until recently, supervising was a task-oriented job. Supervisors spent their days filling out work schedules, giving orders, filing production reports, fielding grievances and evaluating employee performances. They took commands from their superiors and passed them on to their subordinates. They kept their departments organized and efficient, making sure everyone did things right.

Supervisors were the ultimate task managers, often portrayed as burly overseers barking orders and accepting no back talk.

All that has changed. Today's supervisor focuses less on managing tasks and more on leading people toward achievement. They empower their employees. They develop skills and communicate more with their employees than ever before. Today's businesses are asking their supervisors to accept a more demanding role. They need their supervisors to do more than manage tasks; they need them to tap into the organization's most valuable resource — its people. Without the people, there is nothing.

Getting the most from people is crucial in today's intensely competitive business environment. Sharp business leaders have discovered that the world's best plans for cutting costs, increasing quality or modernizing production won't work unless the people within the company are committed to making the strategies work. And smart business leaders rely on supervisors to inspire that commitment among employees.

So, as one of a new breed of supervisors, it's not just your job to make sure things are done; you have to see to it that your people are doing the right things. You have to spark innovation and vision at the grass-roots level, inspiring your employees to look for ways to increase their effectiveness.

You have to be a leader.

Leading Versus Managing

Scenario #1

Bob sits down in the chair across from Suzanne's desk and begins to explain the problem. "I believe the reason this department hasn't met its production quota in three months is because of all the paperwork associated with every order," he tells her. "I'll bet I spend as much time double-checking orders and confirming quantities as I do processing parts through my work station."

Suzanne looks up from her paperwork just long enough to size up Bob's expression. He's a good employee, she thinks to herself, but he's always finding something to gripe about. She responds to him: "I know the paperwork takes up a lot of time, Bob. Look at my desk. But that's the way the execs upstairs want it. They want to keep track of every order and every shred of material that passes through this place. It's all a part of their cost-efficiency program."

Bob says, "I can understand why they want to keep track of all the orders, to reduce waste and mistakes. But there has to be a better system than having all the operators stop what they are doing to fill out a bunch of reports. It's eating up our most productive time."

"I agree," Suzanne says. "But until top management figures out 'a better system,' we're stuck with this system."

*Bob replies, "Can't we just explain to the plant manager that it would make more sense to have one person each day handling all the paperwork? The rest of the team could concentrate on production. That way, work would get done, **and** the paperwork would be taken care of."*

Suzanne stops writing on her report, and says, "Bob, I appreciate your concern. But, the fact is, we're doing things the way the top team wants it done. And none of us has time to go around second-guessing top management or coming up with ways to counteract its poor planning.

"I know you're doing your best. And, I've explained in the monthly reports that my people are working as hard as they can. They know the production problem is not your fault. So, let's just let them figure out a way to handle the paper jam, which they created in the first place, OK?

"I've got too much to do already without spending my afternoon hassling the plant manager about too much paperwork. I have to finish this report on the Thompson account. I've got to start reviewing employee files to prepare my appraisals. I have to organize tomorrow's work assignments. And I told Jamison in accounting I would send over last month's supply costs by tomorrow morning.

"Now is just not a good time for me to be stirring up trouble."

Scenario #2

As he wrapped up his quarterly report, Glenn had to face the fact that the slight drop in production had been more than a figment of his imagination. The figures before him told the whole story. For the first quarter, production in his department had slipped 4.5%.

He had to find the source of the problem.

First, he reviewed all the work orders. They offered no consolation. If his team had kept up with the demand, it would have finished the quarter 5.3% ahead of last year's first quarter.

He reviewed attendance records. He found no clues there, either. Absences and late arrivals were as low as usual. People were on the job. The only trouble was, the work wasn't getting done.

He even talked with other supervisors to see if their teams had experienced similar results for the quarter. A few had matched the previous quarter's production level, but several confessed that they, too, had experienced at least a 4% drop. No one had any answers.

Finally, Glenn went to his employees. Maybe someone on the floor can give me an idea of what's happening, he thought to himself. Most of the meetings he held with employees began with the same chorus, "We're glad you asked...." After talking with individuals and with his people as a group, he began to get a handle on the problem.

Employees were dealing with more breakdowns on the line, and they were producing more defective goods than usual. They were losing time in production, and they were repeating work because of rejected goods.

After doing a little investigating, Glenn discovered that at the beginning of the year the company had started buying raw materials from a new supplier. Evidently, the different material was jamming the company's manufacturing equipment. The problem wasn't a serious one that called immediate attention to itself. Breakdowns and rejections were happening at an almost unnoticeable rate — just steady enough to become a nuisance over a period of time.

After doing a little more investigating, Glenn had enough information to present a proposal to his boss and to the vice president of purchasing. In the proposal, he requested that the company go back to the supplier it had been using formerly.

By the end of the second quarter, the company was back with its old supplier, and soon Glenn's team was back on production schedule.

You don't have to be a management expert to recognize that Glenn was leading while Suzanne was only managing. The difference between the two functions is as big as the difference between giving orders and inspiring people to give their all.

Managing will always be a part of your job. You still have to coordinate work assignments, train your employees, evaluate their performances and handle all those other details that go into running a department. Yet, managing is only a **part** of this role in today's business arena. As the business setting has become more complicated and employees more sophisticated, supervisors have had to become leaders. Beyond telling employees what to do, you must inspire them to do it to the best of their ability. Beyond motivating employees to put their hearts into their work, you need to allow them the freedom and encouragement to use their brains and initiative.

To meet the demands of supervising in the 21st century, you will have to become the kind of person who can guide others, make decisions, and focus on results, not just activities.

I won't tell you that meeting this challenge is easy. For one thing, becoming a leader requires that you examine yourself closely. You will constantly have to review your own attitudes and actions and ask yourself, "Was that the best way to get the results I wanted?" That's more complicated — and often more painful — than it sounds. Self-study requires us to be brutally honest with ourselves and to be willing to criticize our own performances.

Meeting the challenge of becoming a leader also means you will sometimes have to overcome external barriers. Sometimes, top management can get in the way. As much as they want to be flexible, it's also hard for them to change. There will be times when you'll have to have the guts to say to the people over you, "I don't think this is the best way to get the results we want. Maybe this approach would work better...." Changing a business from within can be difficult.

You will also get some resistance from your employees. They have certain attitudes about you, about your position and authority, and about their jobs. As you shift your focus from managing to leading, you will also have to adjust their attitudes. This may be the most difficult aspect of your job. Most employees are used to a certain system. They expect you to give orders and to put them to work. Trying to overcome those expectations and to get them more involved in the planning stages of a project or assignment can seem like moving a mountain.

But let me reassure you that leading a team is not a joyless struggle. You will also find it rewarding.

Satisfaction is a primary reward. As a leader, you will develop a personal sense of purpose that goes beyond getting work done. You will feel called to make a difference.

Positioning yourself as a leader opens the doors of professional advancement. With so few advancement opportunities available, only those rare individuals who get positive results on a consistent basis will see their names on the executive roll.

Dare to accept the leadership challenge, and you will enrich your life. You will find greater satisfaction and rewards on the job, and you will find this success overlapping into your personal life. The qualities that will make you a better leader will make you a better person.

The Second Dimension Of Supervising

In addition to providing a work team with leadership, the job of supervisor also has a less-glamorous, but no-less important, dimension to it. This dimension includes the skills and responsibilities of getting the work done.

Typical responsibilities include:

▶ **Planning and assigning work.**
This usually involves:

❖ Examining organization needs and directives as communicated to you through the command network.

❖ Setting priorities for your team.

❖ Organizing work teams and their assignments for maximum productivity.

▶ **Training and developing employees.**

▶ **Monitoring performance to identify and reinforce positive behavior and results or to identify and correct problems.**

▶ **Maintaining accurate records on your team and its performance and productivity.**

▶ **Acting as liaison between top management and your team.**

▶ **Maintaining a safe work place for employees.**

◗ **Providing employees support needed for accomplishing their assignments and objectives.**

To meet these responsibilities requires certain skills:

◗ **Basic technical skills.** You must understand the specific techniques and procedures your employees use to do the job.

◗ **Human relations skills,** which include several elements:

❖ The ability to communicate effectively with superiors, peers and subordinates.

❖ The ability to tap into employees' motivational drives.

❖ The ability to build positive relationships and to cultivate teamwork.

◗ **Conceptual skills.** You can see and understand the overall operation of the company and your team's role in it, and you can visualize how the components of your plans and actions affect one another. You must see the big picture, without losing sight of the details.

In addition to exploring ways you can develop as a leader, this book also gives you tools necessary for mastering basic people skills.

KEY POINTS

◗ Several factors have brought on the change in responsibility and influence for supervisors:

(1) The rapid pace of change.

(2) The financial squeeze.

(3) A new work ethic.

▶ To meet these demands, supervisors have to be leaders.

▶ Supervisors have to strike a balance between managing the typical supervisory tasks (*such as scheduling assignments, developing employees and reviewing employee performances*) and enabling and inspiring their employees to achieve peak performance.

SELF-DEVELOPMENT STEPS

(1) List any changes within your company that have had a direct impact on your role as supervisor.

(2) Think about ways you could use those changes to develop your leadership role.

2

ALL THE KING'S MEN
Leading Your Team to Achievement

"A creative leader is one who recognizes the potential in people and strives to establish and maintain a climate where individuals may develop and maximize their contributions. Within this creative environment, they involve others in the process of identifying and pursuing meaningful goals that bring both short-term and long-run benefits to all.

— *Robert S. Bailey, Center for Creative Leadership*

In a sense, corporate America is like a giant Humpty Dumpty that fell off its wall of global dominance and needed to be put back together in a creative, competitive way. To the author of the ancient nursery rhyme, reassembling the fragments of an eggshell must have looked like an impossible task, beyond the expertise of all the king's horses and all the king's men.

But American business has learned not to succumb to negative thinking. The need for restructuring to compete in the transnational economy has taken us into the era of downsizing and empowerment of employees at all levels.

By tapping the ingenuity of "all the king's men," a business organization can do more than put Humpty Dumpty back together again; it can make him a healthier, more solid egg than ever before.

But "all the king's men" can't accomplish that prodigious task without leadership. And that's where the modern supervisor comes in.

When they hear the word "leader," most people picture the Alexander the Greats and the Indira Gandhis found on the pages of history textbooks. That's a trap, and understanding the **dynamics of leadership** will help you avoid it. You don't have to conquer an empire or govern a nation or prove your leadership skills through some dramatic struggle or impressive victory.

Leadership is not glitz and glamour. Subtle leadership that gently nudges people to move in the direction you have set for them is as effective (and at least as common) as the brand of leadership that slams its fist on a table and demands action.

Real leadership isn't a matter of dramatics; its main focus is on results. That doesn't mean that leaders can't be dramatic. Some are; it's just a part of their style. But drama is not a prerequisite of leadership.

While I'm shooting down myths, I'd like to add that leaders are not born; they are created — usually by themselves. Whether you consider yourself a "natural-born" leader or believe you will have to work on developing the leadership qualities within you, you have the capacity to lead others to excellence. All of us do. You need only to learn how to tap into that leadership potential.

A Look At Leadership Styles

People have different leadership styles. When I think of the styles I've encountered personally, three men from my Army days come to mind.

The first one I'll call Col. Attila. The name describes the leadership style. He was a dictator — domineering, obnoxious, and arrogant. We didn't have to snap to attention when he walked through the room, but we didn't dawdle either. Col. Attila expected us to be performing full-bore, above and beyond the call of duty.

Col. Attila was later replaced by Col. Deadfish. Col. Deadfish had no personality. He went into his office, closed the door behind him, and disappeared from our screens. He did absolutely nothing in the way of developing us as people.

Then there was Major Galahad. He was a wonderful boss who made a point of helping us develop ourselves as people. He would delegate, but he would also give us the facts and the tools we needed to get the tasks done. He was also a strong motivator. He had an employee-of-the-month program, and he often held wine-and-cheese parties for the staff. His concern for his people was manifested in many ways. If one of us was in the hospital, he was the first one there, with roses or a sympathy card. Major Galahad cared, and it showed.

Colonel Attila, Colonel Deadfish and Major Galahad represent three basic styles into which most leaders fall. They are, respectively, dictators, non-leaders and facilitators. Let's look at each more closely:

CATEGORY #1: *Dictators*

Dictators rule by force. They set policies without consulting anyone, and they expect their people to abide by them without question or input. They want people to follow orders, not share ideas. They demolish egos and crush eggshells to powder.

They discourage feedback, and they expect people to respond to their demands with speed and efficiency. They believe they have to rule with an iron fist to get results. They live by the motto, "If you're not tough with your people, they will take advantage of you. Nobody would ever get anything done if I didn't stay on their backs all the time."

What effect does this approach have on employees? Largely, a negative one.

Dictators usually cripple their employees. They strip them of any sense of initiative. They force dependence. Employees who are never given any freedom or any voice in their work expect management to direct their every step. If they hit a snag or something out of the ordinary happens, they are paralyzed. They've either forgotten how to think for themselves or they are afraid to do so.

Dictators also sow seeds of distrust. Employees can sense when you don't trust them, and they will resent it. If they believe you have no confidence in their ability or their integrity, they will usually become argumentative, aggressive and uncooperative. I believe in the Pygmalion effect — you get what you expect from people. If you expect people to do as little as possible, and you treat them that way, they will do as little as possible. Distrust kills motivation.

Another way to identify dictators is by the way they keep employees powerless. They won't share even the smallest responsibility or the least amount of authority with their employees. They want tight control over every element of their departments. That attitude is dangerous in this day and age.

Powerless employees cannot respond to changes in business or the marketplace. They aren't allowed to innovate. They will not take the initiative to meet a customer's needs or to solve a problem. They will wait until they have specific orders before taking action.

Dictators have to work harder than other leaders, because they refuse to relinquish control. By insisting on dictating every little move, they assume responsibility for every fragment of Humpty Dumpty's shell. Unfortunately, their hard work usually produces poor results. Without the freedom to exercise initiative, all the king's men will find it frustrating and perhaps impossible to put Humpty Dumpty together again.

CATEGORY #2: *Non-leaders*

At the opposite end of the spectrum from dictators are the people I call non-leaders. They have laid-back attitudes toward leading. They let their employees do as they please, hoping everything will fall into place.

Non-leaders give employees little or no guidance. They don't talk to them about company and department objectives. They just hand out daily, weekly or monthly assignments. They never draw connections between company goals and individual employees' goals.

Many times, they let employees choose their own work, without giving any thought to matching the employees to the right jobs.

Managers who fit this description are basically messengers. They transmit orders, requests and comments between their superiors and their subordinates. They give employees just enough information to get the job done. And they don't encourage them to bring their ideas, comments or suggestions to them. They don't want to be bothered with passing along an idea to management.

Employees working for a non-leader are usually frustrated. They often feel ignored. They resent the fact that they are seldom given an opportunity to develop their skills. The employees as a team feel no sense of purpose. No one has ever shown them the connection between their work and the output of the company.

Because they have no clear target for which to aim, employees working for non-leaders seldom perform up to potential. Humpty Dumpty remains a fragmented shell, because nobody provides the leadership and direction needed to reassemble the pieces in the right order.

CATEGORY #3: *Facilitators*

Facilitators are the ideal leaders. They enable, empower and inspire their workers to achieve excellence. They run their departments like a democracy. They involve subordinates in decision-making and encourage them to think for themselves, to be creative and to offer their input. Most people thrive under this style of leadership.

Facilitators treat their employees with respect. They give them responsibility and aren't afraid to transfer control over assignments. How do you think employees respond to this treatment? You guessed it. Nine times out of ten, people who are treated like intelligent, committed adults will respond by acting like intelligent, committed adults.

Facilitators get the best from their employees by giving them a sense of purpose. They understand the importance of drawing concrete connections between employees' personal goals and the objectives of their department.

It's easy to spot a work group that a facilitator leads. The people are organized, energetic and committed to getting positive results — not just to getting the work done. Everyone on the team focuses on achieving their department's objectives, which are always clearly defined.

Facilitators get top-notch results because they do what it takes to maximize their employees' talents, skills and performances. They give their employees the freedom to reach their potential.

They know how to focus the talents and strengths of all the king's men on the task of reassembling Humpty Dumpty.

I hope it's obvious which leadership style is the most effective. The business trend in recent years has been away from strict control and toward more democratic management. Business leaders have learned that getting people involved in their work through participative, democratic management is the best way to tap into their full resources.

Understanding The Qualities Of Leadership

In his book **On Becoming a Leader,** well-known author and consultant Warren Bennis writes: "The process of becoming a leader is much the same as the process of becoming an integrated human being."[2] In other words, it's an on-going practice of self-analysis and self-development. And, it's not easy.

Becoming a leader is not a matter of mastering techniques, as is the case with becoming a pianist or an airplane pilot. Leadership is a state of **being,** not a state of doing. Leading others effectively is not so much a matter of what you do as it is of who you are, what you're all about, and the qualities you possess.

Leaders who have reached the state of being that enables them to inspire others to extraordinary performance possess several qualities:

QUALITY #1: *Self-knowledge*

In their book **Leaders,** Warren Bennis and Burt Nanus quote Theodore Friend III, past president of Swarthmore College: "Leadership is heading into the wind with such **knowledge of oneself** and such collaborative energy as to move others to wish to follow."[3] If you want people to follow you, you have to make them believe that you know not only where you are going but where you stand in relation to that destination. You have to know **you,** your capabilities and limits, your strengths and weaknesses.

To gain self-knowledge, you have to look at yourself candidly. You have to see the flaws and the assets, the dreams and the fears, that are all a part of you and that affect every decision and every action.

QUALITY #2: *Vision*

Very simply, vision is a clear picture of the future a person wants to create. You can't lead the king's men into a reconstruction of Humpty Dumpty unless you help them see what the restored Humpty Dumpty should look like. In a way, vision is a fancy word for a goal. But it's more than a goal, in the sense that it is a driving force. It is an ambition so strong that you will climb over any obstacle; recover from any setback, to turn it into reality.

Without vision, you have nowhere to lead.

QUALITY #3: *Commitment*

Leaders go after their visions with zeal. They are committed to realizing their goals. They are excited about what they are doing, and they infect those around them with enthusiasm.

Without commitment and passion, we are easily distracted from our goals. People soon become disillusioned with our visions. Your employees won't follow you if they sense you are not committed to pursuing your vision.

Commitment to our cause is vital to leadership. It fuels us, and it sparks drive in our followers. We can't lead others to excellence if we have no force to keep us going; if we succumb to the notion that all the king's horses and all the king's men cannot put Humpty Dumpty together again.

QUALITY #4: *Integrity*

Respect is crucial to leadership, and people will respect you only if they are confident in your integrity.

Leaders are honest with themselves, and they are honest with others. They aren't afraid to face facts about themselves or about situations in which they might find themselves.

Leaders also demand that others be honest with them. They want their employees to keep them informed, even if the news is bad. They want to hear negative reviews if one of their strategies or ideas isn't working out.

QUALITY #5: *Curiosity*

Leaders are rarely satisfied with getting only the basic facts. They want to know the why, how, where, when and what of everything.

They wonder about all they see and experience, and are constantly looking for ways to do things better.

QUALITY #6: *Boldness*

Fueled by the strength of their convictions, leaders are willing to take risks in pursuit of their visions. They don't shy away from failure, for they know that mistakes are a part of the learning process.

Their own courage inspires others to take action.

After reading through these brief descriptions of leadership qualities, you must take control of your habits and patterns and shape them so that you become the kind of person and the kind of leader you want to be. You can't just learn a few techniques to become a leader. You have to be willing to change your attitudes and your behavior.

This is quite a challenge, but it's not impossible. And the rewards are endless, both professionally and personally.

You Can Learn To Be A Leader

Earlier I referred to the difference between vested power and real power. Leaders have real power. They don't have to force their employees to strive for top performance. They don't rely on rules or regulations or threats to get action. Leaders influence their workers. They inspire them to give their best, and they guide them in the right direction. This brand of power is the most effective.

People perform for leaders because they want to, not because they have to. When you achieve this "state of being," this inner power, your employees will give their best, whether you are in the office or plant reviewing their progress or are 100 miles away.

The good news is that you can develop this kind of power. You can become a leader. Within each of us is the ability to see ourselves honestly, to focus on a vision, to feel committed, and to hunger to realize our potential as a person. We all can build the character and integrity genuine leadership demands.

Leadership is a learned quality. By that, I mean you can develop leadership qualities. First of all, you can learn to analyze your patterns and your progress. You can take the information available on leadership and apply it to your style and develop in the areas you need to. Once you have the desire to become a leader, you can begin the challenging and rewarding process.

Becoming A Leader: A Continuing Process

As I said earlier, becoming a leader is an on-going, never-ending process. Striving to become a leader is being on an endless mission to progress to a higher level of understanding. I don't think you can reach a certain level of understanding or maturity, then say to yourself, "OK, finally I have all the qualities of a leader. Now I am a great leader." One important quality of leadership, remember, is a continuing desire to grow, to do things better.

You might possess all the leadership qualities we've described, but that doesn't mean you can't continue to grow and improve. For the person committed to becoming a leader by becoming a whole person, it is a life-long process.

A major part of the process is learning from others. Several sources can provide you with a solid education on leadership:

SOURCE #1: *Leaders*

Observe people in all kinds of leadership positions.

Identify effective leaders and try to determine what they are doing right. But don't overlook the poor leaders. You can learn a lot from them by determining what they are doing wrong.

Think of bosses you've had. Did any of them have a knack for uniting their teams and accomplishing their objectives? What worked for them? If possible, find a leadership mentor, someone who can help you understand the finer points of leadership. Such persons can guide you in the right direction. They can give you honest advice, and they can answer your questions. They can share with you the benefit of their experience.

Don't limit yourself just to the people you know or who are directly connected to you somehow. We can find leadership examples everywhere. You can learn a lot about leadership by watching the President of the United States, for example, or any world or government leader. Read news articles. What kind of reviews are these people getting, and why? Always ask yourself what you can learn from them.

Keep up with business news. Which business leaders are being hailed as heroes, and who is being labeled as a loser? What can you learn from their experiences? What are they doing that is drawing so much fire from critics?

Observe other leaders, and soak up the lessons they offer.

SOURCE #2: *Other people*

Leaders aren't the only people who can help you develop your leadership skills. You can learn by watching and relating to all kinds of people.

The relationships you have with the people you hope to influence and guide are at the heart of leadership. And tuning into the people you want to lead is one of the best ways I know for learning about how to influence them. By getting to them and paying attention to them, you can identify and respond to their needs and drives; to their individual perceptions and ways of relating.

As you get to know them, your employees can tell you a great deal about how to tap into their inner resources. You just have to pay attention to them and listen to their needs. Throughout this book, we'll be discussing ways you can get to know your employees, build strong relationships with them and motivate them to peak performance.

SOURCE #3: *Books and other educational materials*

You'd be amazed at the ideas you can find in books and magazines that can help you stay on top of your industry and on top of the latest trends in leadership and business.

It is a good idea to keep up with trends and new schools of thought involving leadership. Just as becoming a leader is not a one-time shot, neither is the process of defining the ideal leader. As we learn more about people, we continue to refine our ideas about who is a model leader.

In addition to checking out articles, books and cassette tapes on the topic of leadership, it can be helpful to read biographies of successful leaders. Studying their lives and their approaches to responsibilities and to the people they lead can broaden your understanding of what it takes to lead others to excellence.

SOURCE #4: *Your own experience*

Learning is a process of trial and error, no matter what area you're studying. It's no different than becoming a leader. Sometimes you'll make the right decision, take the appropriate action, and feel satisfied you did something right.

Other times, you will misjudge a situation, react with haste or overlook vital details, and create dissension among your ranks. Learn from these experiences, both the good and the bad.

Leadership: An Integral Part Of You

As you increase your self-awareness and your commitment to self-development and excellence, the ability to lead will naturally grow within you. Leadership is more a **result** of pursuing self-actualization (which is basically what we've been talking about throughout this chapter — developing yourself as a person, not just as a supervisor) than a **cause** in itself.

As you become an integrated person, you open yourself to the challenges that give you the opportunity to achieve and to lead others to achievement. When you reach this level of self-actualization, you can use your talents and energies fully, and you can inspire the people around you to fulfill their potential. With this kind of leadership, you're not limited by your own knowledge and abilities. You have the strengths and talents of all the king's men — and women — behind you.

Key Points

▶ You can divide most leaders into one of three basic categories.

(1) Dictators.

(2) Non-leaders.

(3) Facilitators.

▶ Becoming a leader is not a matter of mastering techniques, in the manner of learning to play the piano or to fly a plane. Leadership is a state of being, not a state of doing. It is an on-going process of self-analysis and self-development.

▶ Leaders who have reached a state of being that enables them to inspire others to extraordinary performance share several qualities:

(1) Self-knowledge.

(2) Vision.

(3) Commitment.

(4) Integrity.

(5) Curiosity.

(6) Boldness.

▶ A major part of becoming a leader is learning from others. Several sources can provide you with a solid education on leadership:

(1) Leaders.

(2) Other people.

(3) Books and other educational materials.

(4) Your own experience.

Self-Development Steps

(1) Inventory the leadership qualities you believe you now possess.

(2) List areas in which you would like to improve.

3

THE RESPONSIBLE EGO
Getting Power Through Empowerment

"There is a quiet revolution taking place in many organizations. The source of the revolution is the growing realization that tighter controls, greater pressure, more clearly defined jobs, and tighter supervision have, in the last 50 years, run their course in their ability to give us the productivity gains we require to compete effectively in the world marketplace. Attention is shifting to the need for employees to personally take responsibility for the success of our businesses if we hope to survive and prosper." [4]

— Peter Block, author **The Empowered Manager**

Becoming a leader is a self-oriented endeavor. The process centers on you — everything you do, you think, you are. It is wrapped around developing **you.**

That means that the leader must have an ego — a strong sense of confidence and pride in oneself. Leading, however, is an "other-centered" activity. That is, it's an undertaking that, by definition, focuses on others, influencing them to take a certain action or behave in a particular way. So true leadership also calls for a responsible ego — one that takes into account the talents, strengths and egos of others.

No matter what qualities I possess, I am a leader only if others follow me of their free will. I might have integrity and vision, conviction and courage, but those virtues won't get the work done unless I have inspired **and enabled** my team to perform.

The Power Of Empowerment

The "quiet revolution," to which Peter Block refers in the introduction to his book **The Empowered Manager,** is causing a drastic power shift within many organizations. The demands of the new business environment — rapid change, downsizing, a new work ethic — are forcing managers to get employees on all levels to accept responsibility for the operation and success of their companies.

To do that, managers have had to adjust their authoritarian attitudes. They have had to give employees not only the tools and information needed for doing a job, but also the authority to adapt and innovate as necessary. They have learned that strict supervision doesn't work in an environment where flexibility and responsiveness are the keys to corporate survival.

Some supervisors still reject the idea of giving more power to employees. They believe that any power they transfer to employees means less power for themselves. This is not the attitude of a responsible ego. It is a misconception that has stunted more than a few supervisors' careers. Power is not a fixed property. Giving someone else power doesn't mean you are left with less.

In reality, about the only way supervisors, or any managers, for that matter, can maximize their power is to empower their employees. You don't increase your power by holding on to all decision-making responsibilities or telling people every move to make. You boost your power by producing positive results. And to get positive results in today's complex business arena, you have to share responsibilities and **authority.** Every employee must be willing **and able** to respond immediately to problems, changes and customer needs.

Empowering your employees is not giving up your role as leader; it is strengthening it. By loosening your controls over employees, you free them — and yourself — to accomplish more.

Empowered employees are less dependent on you. They won't feel that they have to consult with you on every move they make.

Empowered employees have the freedom to experiment and innovate — and to make mistakes. At a time when innovation has become the weapon of choice in the struggle to stay ahead of the competition, this freedom is vital.

Empowered employees support each other, which is critical in a management-lean organization. You probably feel that there isn't enough of you to go around. One solution to that problem is to cultivate cooperation among your employees. Encourage them to go to one another for help and information when they can.

Empowered employees will take the initiative. When they see that something needs to be done, they'll take care of it. If they have a solution to a problem, they'll implement it.

Empowered employees are more committed to their jobs. They feel a personal sense of responsibility for their work and the results they produce.

Empowered employees need less supervision. You, then, can devote your energies to leading your team rather than managing it.

Supervisors become more powerful as they nurture the power in the people on their work teams. When you empower your employees, you create a team of people who have the ability and the desire to respond to unpredictable events. You create a team of people who can respond to changes in the industry and who work with energy and a commitment to the company's goals.

How To Empower

We've used the word "empowerment" quite a bit so far in this book and talked about the importance of giving your employees power. But, what is empowerment, really? How exactly do you **give** power to someone?

Think about your personal experiences. Maybe you've worked in a situation in which you felt you had a vote; people listened to you and gave you credit for being an intelligent, thinking human being. How did you feel in that situation? You probably felt energized, as if you could make a difference through your work. If so, you have some idea of what it is to be empowered.

Feeling empowered depends basically on three elements:

▶ **Having control of your fate**. Empowered people understand that they alone are responsible for the successes and failures in their lives — whether it's on the job or at home. They don't blame circumstances for their situations. They know that happiness and success are up to them, regardless of what's happening.

▶ **Having a purpose**. Most people today want more than a job; more than a way to pay the bills. They want to feel that their work contributes to something bigger than the family income. They want to feel needed; to have a reason for living.

▶ **Being committed to that purpose.** Empowered people pursue their purposes regardless of the support — or lack of it — they receive from their environment. They don't wait for the right boss or the perfect working conditions to give their best to reach their goals; they are committed to fulfilling their purposes, driven by their desire to make a difference.

I need to make an important point here: Although you can empower your employees, the feeling of empowerment must come from within them. You can create the conditions that favor empowerment, but your employees must take active roles in accepting power.

Unfortunately, most employees don't come automatically equipped with a sense of power or a willingness to accept it. You have to remember that it's only been in the last decade or so that managers have recognized the importance of tapping into their employees' full potential. Many of your employees work within the mind set that you are the boss; you give orders and they follow them. They might not like this arrangement, but that's the way it's always been, and they have no reason to expect it to change.

One of the toughest jobs you face as an empowering supervisor is to help employees make the adjustment from waiting for orders to accepting power and using it in constructive ways. You can't simply walk into a meeting and say to your people, "I've decided you people will get more work done if you are given more autonomy. From now on, I want you to make decisions on your own, to take some initiative in solving problems and responding to customer needs, and to implement innovative ways to increase our productivity and beat the competition." You would probably end up with chaos.

Peter Block captures the concept of empowerment perfectly: "The primary task of supervision is to help people trust their own instincts and take responsibility for the success of the business."[5]

Helping your people move into the new role that today's business environment demands of all employees can be a challenging experience. It is worth the trouble, though, and it can be done. Here is a set of strategies the supervisor with a responsible ego can use to help employees make the transition to empowerment:

STRATEGY #1: *Develop your people*

To get employees to "trust their instincts" you must build their confidence. That means equipping your employees with the right knowledge and the right attitudes to do their jobs to the best of their abilities. If you want your people to feel empowered, develop their skills and talents.

There are several ways to build your employees' confidence in their skills:

▶ **Develop your employees' skills.** When I say "skills," I'm talking about the technical skills needed to do the job and the basic job skills that enable employees to take full advantage of their opportunities.

To build technical skills, give your employees challenging assignments that will expand their abilities.[6] Don't give people the same work all the time. Cross-train your employees on all the jobs in your shift or department.

When I talk about basic job skills, I mean such things as decision-making, creative thinking and innovativeness. Teach your employees to use their minds. Ask them for input. Present them with problems and ask for solutions.

Don't expect immediate results. Remember, they are used to bringing you their problems, not solving them themselves.

▶ **Lead by example.** Model the behavior you want from your employees. People will react more to what you do than to what you **say.** If your words and actions don't match, your integrity will be jeopardized.

If you want your employees to be committed to their work, be committed to your work. If you want them to be committed to the company, be committed to the company. If you want them to be committed to you, then you be committed to them.

If you want your employees to share your sense of purpose, share with them your vision for the department and for the company. Talk to them in specifics, explaining the roles you would like each of them to fill in your vision for the department. And, encourage them to develop their own visions. Ask them to imagine where they see themselves in the future at your company.

Spark your employees' enthusiasm and tap into their energies by igniting a sense of purpose within them. Show them that they have more than a job; they have a mission.

▶ **Respect your employees.** You will not build a person's confidence if you don't treat that person with respect. Make your employees feel valuable.

Treating employees with respect means that you assume that they are *honest, intelligent and dedicated*. Let your treatment of them reflect that assumption.

I have found that people respond positively to positive attitudes. Don't be constantly checking up on your employees, questioning their motives and expecting them to goof off.

Most employees are hard workers and resent being spied on or treated like school children playing hooky. If they believe you don't trust them, they will be reluctant to accept additional responsibilities, primarily because they won't trust you.

▶ **Maintain openness**. Talk to your employees. Let them know what's happening in their department. Make them feel "in on" things. Knowledge is power, and informed employees are empowered employees.

Be open with your employees about the challenges you face as a team. Let them know that you need their support, because you do. And they can only give you their support if they know what is going on.

▶ **Be a consultant to your subordinates.** As I said, you can't just tell your employees you want them to take on more responsibilities and then abandon them. As you give your employees more freedom, let them know that you are on hand to assist them. Be willing to spend time with them and to advise them how to do what they do better. Offer them support. Just be careful not to take over their problems or assignments.

STRATEGY #2: *Build ways to empower people*

In addition to building your employees' confidence and helping to develop the skills that enable them to perform at peak capacity, you have to design ways that encourage their full participation in the operation of your department.

For example, if you expect your employees to lean on each other more, create open environments that encourage them to work jointly. Have employees do projects together.

Here are a couple of additional tips for building an empowering environment:

▶ **Be accessible.** Let employees know that you want to hear from them. Encourage them to bring you their ideas and opinions. Explore their attitudes and feelings toward changes in the department or company.

▶ **Use participative decision-making.** Have employee meetings to address issues affecting your department. Ask your employees for suggestions and input.

▶ **Supervise by invitation only.** A wise person once said, "The best executive is the one who has sense enough to pick good people to do what he wants done, and self-restraint enough to keep from meddling with them while they do it."[7]

This may be something you have to work up to. But once you have cultivated a strong team of people who are willing to accept responsibility, give them room. Give an assignment, then back out of the picture. Be on hand for guidance or assistance, but don't get deeply involved in the project. Unless you see a serious problem developing, wait for your employees to come to you if they hit a snag.

Supervising by invitation has several benefits. First, it shows your employees that you have faith in their abilities and their professionalism. Your actions say to them, "I know you can do what needs to be done, and I trust you will follow through on this responsibility without my constantly looking over your shoulder."

Second, when you are able to give your employees this much freedom, you have more time and energy to devote to your responsibilities.

Everyone is better off.

STRATEGY #3: *Learn to let go of control*

Supervisors in the old days had a reputation for being the drill sergeants of the work place. For some of you, I am asking you to make major changes in your approach to your job. Remember, however, that control is not power.

I'm not asking you to relinquish power. I'm simply suggesting that you allow your employees to reach their potential and achieve peak performance. They can't do that as long as you are pulling in the reins on them.

What can you do to loosen your grip on control? Here are several tips:

▶ Supervise, rather than do. When you give an assignment, step back and let your people do the work.

▶ Know when to include your team in a decision. You can't possibly know everything about everything that is happening in your department. Get the people working involved in decisions.

Let them know that they bring a unique perspective to the decision-making process that improves the quality of the final solution.

In addition to involving your team, don't avoid making decisions or put off making them. Face them as soon as they come up. Decisiveness is essential to good management.

▶ **Admit it when you don't know something.** I know some supervisors who are afraid that if they admit they don't have all the answers, they will lose their employees' respect. No one expects you to know everything. You stand more of a chance of losing people's respect if you come across as an egotistical phony who has all the answers or who can never accept anyone else's input.

When faced with a problem or dilemma, survey your team for someone who might have the right knowledge or information. This approach builds individual team members' confidence and taps a large pool of information and knowledge resources.

▶ **Delegate effectively.** How, what, why, when and to whom you delegate can have a tremendous impact on your workers' confidence and abilities. Learn to delegate in a way that builds employees' strengths and helps them overcome their weaknesses.

▶ **Accept conflict as a healthy part of teamwork.** Some people equate peace with prosperity. That's not always true in business. This anonymous quote makes my point wonderfully: "When two people in business always agree, one of them is unnecessary."[8]

Where there is intelligent debate, based on accurate information and careful thought, you have a vital business that is open to growth and improvement. When you encourage people to think for themselves and to innovate, you are bound to have some conflicts. People will have their own ideas. And if they believe in them, they will fight for them.

This kind of constructive conflict keeps fresh ideas circulating throughout an organization.

▶ **Offer frequent and sincere praise.** If you want your employees to feel good about their work and about themselves, be generous with praise. Whenever employees do good or outstanding jobs, let them know that you've noticed.

Your praise should always be genuine. No one likes to be patronized.

Handing out undeserved compliments waters down all your congratulations, whether or not they are genuine. After a while, people won't value your cheers, even when they are sincere.

Key Points

▶ Empowering your employees is not giving up your role as a leader; it is strengthening it. By loosening your controls over employees, you free them — and yourself — to accomplish more.

▶ Feeling empowered depends basically on three elements:

(1) Controlling your fate.

(2) Knowing you have a purpose.

(3) Being committed to that purpose.

▶ One of the toughest jobs you face as an empowering supervisor is to help employees make the adjustment from playing a passive role in your department's operation to accepting power and using it in constructive ways. Use these strategies to help employees make the transition to empowerment:

(1) Develop your people.

(2) Build systems that empower people.

(3) Learn to let go of control.

Self-Development Steps

(1) What do you consider the most challenging aspect of empowering your employees? List any areas in which you find it difficult to relinquish control.

(2) Examine your reasons for not giving your employees more freedom, and look for ways you can increase their responsibilities in the most productive way.

4

HAM RADIOS AND SMOKE SIGNALS
Communicating Clearly

"Acts of communication can be described as the thread that holds any social organization together, if not the skeleton that determines its structure."

— Ithiel de Sola Pool

Effective communication within an organization is **the** critical function that energizes and controls all others.

Without communication, you have no organization. You may have a group of people working near each other, but they don't make up an organization until they join together to accomplish a common objective.

A company is an organization because it produces results through a system of interpersonal and interdepartmental connections.

▶ Company heads communicate with their staff and employees on all levels, with customers, and with outside resources, so they can keep in touch with changes and trends and steer their companies through today's turbulent business waters.

▶ Managers on every level communicate with one another, with superiors and with subordinates to organize projects and activities in a way that guarantees consistently high productivity.

▶ Rank-and-file employees communicate with superiors to spell out directives and make suggestions; they communicate among themselves to develop the most effective methods and systems for accomplishing their objectives; and they provide a vital link to customers. Effective communication skills are crucial for identifying and relaying to management customers' needs and wants. In today's competitive environment, customer contact is a critical business responsibility.

A company depends on the circulation of information to survive, much as the human body depends on the circulation of blood. For a company to use its resources fully, individuals on all levels must have the skills and the freedom to share information and ideas openly .

As a supervisor, you have a demanding role in maintaining clear communication within the organization. You have to communicate with your employees, your peers and your superiors in a way that builds understanding, high morale and achievement. You are the connecting link between upper management and the ranks you supervise. You are expected to receive, understand and accurately transmit messages back and forth between your superiors and your subordinates.

If that sounds like a complicated job to you, you're right. Communicating effectively is as difficult as it is important. Becoming a skilled communicator, however, will have a tremendous impact on your ability to reach peak performance and to lead your team to maximum productivity.

Understanding Communication

Most dictionaries define communication as "the act of transmitting" or "a giving or exchanging of information, signals or messages by talk, gestures, writing, etc."[9] That description, however, barely scratches the surface of what it means to communicate effectively.

There are all kinds of ways of transmitting messages, and all kinds of signals that convey information. You can use everything from smoke signals to satellite relays.

If your town has been demolished by an earthquake, you may find it useful to spell out an SOS in smoke signals from the burning rubble. But if you need rescue helicopters, cranes and bulldozers; if you need penicillin, morphine, and bandages, you're better off with a ham radio operator who can send out a clear, explicit, message.

Much of what passes for communication in our society comes in the form of smoke signals — hazy, coded, non-verbal messages that are not always easy to decipher.

Do any of the following scenarios demonstrate effective communication?

▶ A salesperson walks up to a customer in a store and says, "Can I help you?" The customer responds that she is only looking.

▶ A manager says to an employee, "You're not working fast enough. You're going to have to keep pace with the rest of the team or we're going to have to do something about it." The employee says he will try harder.

▶ Management posts a memo on the bulletin board: "We have just landed a major contract with ACME Co. Everyone's cooperation will be required to make this business relationship a success."

Which interchanges are effective? None of them. People are talking. They are transmitting and receiving messages. Yet the people involved are not connecting. They are not moving toward a greater understanding of one another through their exchanges. They are communicating with smoke signals.

The "Can-I-help-you?-No-I'm-just-looking" tango, for instance, is a form of communication that most of us have mastered for those times when we want to **avoid** sharing information.

In the second scenario, just what does the supervisor mean by "do something about it"? Is the supervisor going to fire the employee, transfer him to another department or give him special training? And, what does "try harder" mean? Is the employee going to ask co-workers for tips on speeding up? Is he going to sacrifice quality for speed? Is he going to make others slow down so his pace doesn't seem slow? Neither person in this scenario expressed exactly what he meant.

In the third scenario, management creates a lot of questions by suggesting that "cooperation" will be the key to success in a new business venture. Employees might interpret that as an accusation that they don't cooperate now. Or maybe they will read that note and worry that management expects them to work harder and longer hours with little or no additional compensation. Vague memos from management can stir up strong negative feelings.

Communication is obviously much more than sending and receiving messages. And in business, miscommunication can result in more than an occasional lost sale as well as in mixed feelings now and then.

To supervise a team of employees for maximum productivity, you have to learn to get beyond empty phrases or words. You have to make connections with people. Like ham radio operators trying to make communication with each other, you have to establish a common frequency. To make a connection means that you strive to make yourself understood and you focus on understanding the people you communicate with. You don't exchange words; you exchange meanings.

When you communicate effectively, you connect with your employees in a way that builds teamwork and enhances productivity. Communicating for better understanding doesn't simply involve words; it's a way of doing things. And as with leadership, it's a way of being. It's an attitude.

For example, let's say you have a work order for your staff members. You could say to them, "You have to produce 1,500 units in one week. That means everyone will have to work two hours overtime every night this week. Get to work." That might be within your rights as a supervisor. But, would that be the most effective way to handle the situation?

A more effective approach would be something like this: "I have a work order here stating that we have to produce 1,500 units by Friday for McPherson Trucking, one of our biggest and most important customer accounts. We can do it if everyone is willing to work two hours overtime every night this week. Or maybe there are some other options. Does anybody have any ideas?"

The first method of giving orders devalues employees, treats them like robots and fails to take advantage of their skill and intelligence. The second approach respects the workers' abilities and capacity to think. It builds teamwork with the use of the word "we," and taps into all the employees' resources, including the brainpower to come up with a plan to complete the project on time.

It's easy to see that communicating effectively on the corporate level is more complicated than simply talking or giving orders. It's trying to achieve a level of understanding with others that helps them perform better and, therefore, increases productivity. Accomplishing this feat is not easy.

Facing The Complications Of Communication

It has been estimated that 70% of business communication doesn't achieve its purpose. That's a lot of miscommunication. And there's a lot more at stake in business communication than hurt feelings or an occasional innocent mishap in production. Breakdowns in communication can cost companies thousands, in some cases even hundreds of thousands, of dollars each year.

In his book, **The Believable Corporation,** Roger D'Aprix, tells a story about failed communication that was costing a products company approximately $200,000 a month.[10]

A welder at Superba Products Company told her supervisor that a large number of containers she was responsible for sealing were failing quality control tests. Jane informed her boss, Ed, that she discovered a common factor with all the rejected containers — small white spots on their backsides. Jane explained to Ed that if she removed these white spots before welding, the containers would go through testing without any glitches.

Ed's response was to remind Jane that she was a welder, not a quality-control inspector. All she had to do was seal the boxes, not worry about solving quality-control problems. But, Jane wasn't so easily dissuaded. She approached the quality- control supervisor with her discovery. She suggested that, if his crew would remove the white spots before testing, the rejection rate would probably drop considerably. The QC supervisor looked over his work order, then told Jane that he and his crew had no instructions for cleaning white spots off the containers.

Jane decided to take another route. She looked for the source of the white spots and found it in an early manufacturing step. Workers were taking the still-hot containers as they came out of furnaces and putting them on white cooling trays. The trays melted and stuck to the metal. So Jane simply asked the production supervisor to stop using the plastic trays for cooling.

The production supervisor had an attitude similar to the quality-control manager's. He informed Jane he had orders to use the cooling trays and she needed to mind her own business. If that wasn't demoralizing enough, the production supervisor complained to Ed, Jane's supervisor, who then blasted her for pestering other departments.

Jane reluctantly gave up her quest to solve the problem. The best she could do, she decided, was to scrape the white spots when she had time. The rejection rate on the containers, however, remained high.

That would be the end of the story, except that the company had a job-enrichment program which included random meetings between employees and the plant manager. When Jane's turn for a "coffee conference" came around, she told him the whole story about the containers and the white dots. The plant manager was the only one who listened to Jane and discovered she had the solution to a problem that was costing the company an estimated $2.4 million a year.[11]

Certainly, that's a dramatic example of the financial drain poor communications can have on a business. This story, however, illustrates vividly the difficulty of making yourself heard and understood within the walls of a business. Many times the systems within the organization seem designed to block communication rather than assist it.

Supervisors, and their employees as well, face several obstacles when trying to communicate with and relate to the people with whom they work. I have found that both internal and external barriers block our attempts to communicate.

Internal barriers can be the most difficult obstacles to overcome in the communication process, because they are hard to recognize and remedy. Here are several common internal barriers we all have to deal with:

INTERNAL BARRIER #1: *Differing perceptions*

Most of the individuals in a work place come from different backgrounds. They each have experienced life differently, and these experiences have shaped their ambitions, attitudes, value systems and perceptions.

For example, I grew up in a somewhat close-knit family. I see and respond to the world differently from a person who has no family ties. I am ambitious, but my primary goal is to help people reach their potential. I react to the events in my life differently from the way a person who would react who values personal accomplishments more highly than helping others.

Differences in perception, even on a small scale, can create barriers to understanding. One employee might respond positively to being left alone to do his work. He enjoys the freedom. Another employee with similar skills might perceive being left alone as being ignored. To this person, the supervisor is neglecting her and failing to encourage her development.

To communicate effectively, you have to be sensitive to the fact that people interpret the messages you send according to their perceptions and points of view. You have to respond to your employees as individuals and to make sure you understand their perceptions and they understand yours.

Until people's perceptions match, they cannot communicate effectively.

INTERNAL BARRIER #2: *Expectations*

Our expectations often block the real message someone is trying to convey.

The supervisor expects her employees to accept job directives without objection, so she doesn't know how to respond when one person complains about a demanding work order.

A company executive expects a business partner to support his ideas during a board meeting and completely misses the point of the partner's message when he starts debating with him on a critical issue.

Our expectations, as well as our perceptions, shade our understanding of what others are telling us. We can lose the entire meaning of another person's message when we focus on what we **expect** him or her to say.

INTERNAL BARRIER #3: Prejudices and notions

Prejudices and preconceived notions can clutter our minds so that we are unable to accept information or messages from others. Some people in upper management have been accused of turning a deaf ear on lower-rank employees. They are suspected of discounting any suggestions from the front lines as simplistic and of no use in the **real** business world. Countless good ideas fall into a black hole in the business universe because a manager didn't believe his or her employees could offer insight into a problem or situation.

Open your mind, and listen to your employees — listen to understand. Don't look for the problems with an idea or piece of information. Look for the reasons the person sharing it with you thinks it's valuable.

INTERNAL BARRIER #4: *Selectivity*

We're all guilty of hearing only what we want to hear. For example, most of us just want to hear good news. Unfortunately, that's not a smart way to run a business or a department. You have to open your ears to all information, ideas and feedback.

Certainly, we have to be selective, to some degree, in what we listen to. Dozens of sources of information try to get our attention. If we were to pay attention to all the noise coming from various media and all the people around us, we'd go berserk. To defend ourselves against insanity, most of us have learned to tune in to only what we choose to hear.

This defense is helpful — until we start inadvertently tuning out useful information. We can get into the habit of ignoring people or information that doesn't reinforce our beliefs and policies. We reduce our effectiveness as communicators when we close our minds for any reason.

INTERNAL BARRIER #5: *Preoccupation*

If you have 20 things to do before the end of the day, you might have difficulty focusing on the messages others are trying to send you. Having too many things on your mind can also make it difficult for you to express yourself clearly. You may feel as if you don't have time to organize your thoughts. Or while you're addressing one issue, your mind is on another, so you jumble your messages.

All the details of managing a team for maximum productivity crowd into your mind and get in the way of sending and receiving messages accurately. To communicate effectively, you have to learn to concentrate and to boot out thoughts that have nothing to do with the topic of discussion.

INTERNAL BARRIER #6: *Emotions and attitudes*

The way we feel can have a tremendous impact on how receptive we are to others' messages. Anger, for example, is a strong barrier to communication. Think of a time when you've been angry with another person. Did you really want to listen to what he or she said to you? More than likely, all you could think about was venting your anger, regardless of the results.

Emotions also make it difficult for us to express ourselves clearly. Fear, anger or disappointment get in the way of organizing our thoughts or focusing on someone else's messages.

If you've ever run into any of these barriers when you were trying to communicate with others, it might make you feel better to know that everyone is susceptible to them. We are only human, after all. Emotions, perceptions and prejudices are a part of our being. At one time or another, at least one of these monsters is going to rear up and cause confusion.

The key to avoiding these barriers is to be aware of them. Many times, knowing that they are lurking within every exchange of communication enables you to prevent them altogether. You can take steps to match people's perceptions. You can learn to keep your emotions in check. You can identify your prejudices and preconceived notions. And you can be aware that other people are dealing with the same internal distractions, and express yourself in a way that avoids confusion. In spite of these barriers, you can communicate effectively.

The internal obstacles, however, are not the only barriers to understanding. We must also contend with outside interference.

EXTERNAL BARRIER #1: Interruptions

In today's overcommunicative society, it's almost impossible to have a conversation or discussion without interruption. Even when you're meeting in an office, you have to deal with people knocking on the door or buzzing you on the telephone. If you're on the telephone, pulsating tones and flashing lights call your attention to another call.

Communicating effectively demands that you think about what you are saying and what others are saying to you. Even occasional interruptions can destroy the concentration needed to achieve understanding with others.

EXTERNAL BARRIER #2: Distractions

Often something catches our eye outside a window or door, a noise makes it impossible to hear what someone is saying, or a nearby conversation grabs our attention. Even our own thoughts can divert our attention away from our conversations or discussions. We start thinking about an afternoon meeting with our boss. Or we worry about filling the production quota for the week. As our thoughts wander, we miss the meaning of what another person is telling us or we lose our train of thought.

These distractions are similar to static on a radio. The signal is coming through, but interference cuts down the clarity of the message.

EXTERNAL BARRIER #3: Environmental conditions

Have you ever attended a conference or seminar where the room was stuffy? No matter how interesting a speaker is or how interested you are in a topic being discussed, certain environmental conditions affect the way we feel and our ability to pay attention.

A warm room after lunch puts us to sleep. A room that's too cold can have a similar effect. Chairs that are too soft can make us relax and start daydreaming. A chair that's too uncomfortable can distract our attention from a discussion as we look for the least-painful sitting position.

A good rule to remember is that the ideal environment for communicating is neither too relaxing nor too uncomfortable. An environment that doesn't call attention to itself is the least distracting.

You Can Communicate Effectively

The odds against breaking through all those barriers — both internal and external — and making yourself understood might seem overwhelming. The truth of the matter is, as I stated earlier, failed communication is more common than successful communication in the business setting. But, that doesn't mean you're doomed to misunderstandings and miscommunications.

Tapping into your team's full potential is possible, once you recognize the importance of effective communication, acknowledge the barriers you face, and master a few simple guidelines for improving your communication skills.

Guideline #1: *Be aware of your impact on others*

Communication is not an activity that can be separated from leading or supervising a team. It's an integral part of everything a supervisor — or any person in any position, for that matter — does. Everything about you communicates, if not a message, at least an attitude.

The way you interact with others, the way you give assignments, the way you respond to your employees' needs, the way you handle directives from upper management, the priorities you place on tasks — all these elements have an impact on your effectiveness as a communicator. The old adage that actions speak louder than words is true. Your conduct and attitude color the meanings of your words.

If you walk past your employees in the morning without saying hello, you've communicated with them. If you sit down for lunch with your crew, you convey a feeling. If you keep your door closed all day, coming out only to give an order or to check up on someone's work, you might as well flash a "do-not-disturb" sign. If you ask for worker input, you communicate an interest in your employees' ideas and opinions.

Recognizing the impact your actions and attitudes have on the messages you send is vital to improving your effectiveness as a communicator.

Guideline #2: *Understand the forms of communication*

Communication occurs on several levels in the work place. Information is transmitted along formal and informal lines of communication.

Formal communication follows established procedures and focuses on work-related issues. Memos, reports, in-house newsletters and written directives are part of the formal communication system. Speeches by members of upper management are another example of formal communication.

Formal communications are most effective for getting specific information to large numbers of people. If a company has an announcement affecting the entire organization, it's simpler to present the information in a standard form so everyone receives the same data.

Informal communication covers just about all other interactions at work. It's unplanned and follows no set procedures. A group standing around the coffee machine on break discussing the newest piece of equipment is informal communication. A one-on-one conversation with an employee is informal communication. The grapevine is part of an organization's informal communication network. It can be a useful part of the network, or it can be a fountain of negative misinformation, depending upon how open a company is with its employees.

As I was working with a group of supervisors in a chemical company, I encountered an interesting example of a grapevine gone wild.

Frank, a quiet man who had spoken very little during the session, raised his hand and told us a story. Frank had slipped and fallen at work, but it was nothing serious — until the news hit the grapevine.

By the end of the day, you could take your choice:

❱ Frank had slipped and broken his back.
❱ He had severed his hip joint.
❱ He had broken his femur.
❱ He was unconscious and was sent to the hospital.

In any case, according to the grapevine, Frank had only a few hours to live. In fact, he was quite healthy and sound. The flurry of misinformation started when his supervisors shut down the source of accurate information. When people asked what happened to Frank, they were told, "Oh, I don't need to tell you."

The grapevine is employees' attempt to understand and make sense of their environment. If they don't have access to all the information they need, employees will start filling in the gaps with guesses and assumptions. As long as it's carrying accurate information, the grapevine is not necessarily a bad thing in an organization. It keeps people connected. No matter what's happening at a company or how effective the lines of formal communication are, employees will cultivate a grapevine. People like to talk about what they have in common, so it only makes sense that co-workers talk about work.

The best way to be sure the grapevine is building positive communication and productivity is to be open with employees. Don't withhold information from them and make them guess what's happening in the company. Keep them informed.

In addition to formal and informal communication, you also have upward and downward communication (which are exactly what they sound like) and horizontal communication. Downward communication goes from top to bottom, and it's the most common form of dispatch within a company. It's only natural that executives write policies and directives that filter their way down through the ranks. A progressive company, however, recognizes the importance of encouraging and cultivating upward and horizontal communication.

Management needs to hear from the people on the front lines, whether they are in production or sales. And, employees on every level can share solutions by communicating laterally.

If you, as a supervisor, want to have access to all the information you need to run your department most effectively, encourage upward communication.

▶ **Invite and reinforce frank and open discussions with and among your employees.**

▶ **Respond positively to bad news as well as good, so your employees feel comfortable sharing everything with you.**

▶ **Redefine the open-door policy. Take the initiative and walk through the door to associate with your employees. You don't have to wait for them to come to you.**

▶ **Build trust with your employees. Don't condemn or criticize them for their ideas. Don't betray people's trust; keep private matters private. Give credit where it is due when your employees share good ideas.**

Guideline #3: *Keep the lines of communication open*

Talk to your employees. Let them know what is happening within your department and throughout the company. Informed employees are empowered employees. They have the knowledge necessary to make intelligent judgments and decisions.

Keeping your employees informed is an excellent strategy for motivating them and getting them involved in the operation of the company — not just "getting the work done." When you share information freely with your employees, they feel "in on" things, which is important. We all like to be part of an "in" group. If your employees sense that they are not privy to company news or data, they will feel disconnected from the organization. That's no way to promote dedication and teamwork.

Guideline #4: *Messages that build understanding*

Although communication goes deeper than words, you can follow a few pointers for getting your message across accurately.

▶ **Make sure you have the attention of the people you're communicating with.** No worthwhile communication takes place until you gain the complete attention of the people you're speaking to. Attention and response are the only things that turn words and images into communication.

The most effective way to get and keep listeners' attention is to phrase your messages in a way that the people you're talking with can see how the information relates to them. Talk about what is important to them, and talk to them on their level. And pay attention to their responses to judge their level of interest or the direction in which to take the conversation.

▶ **Organize your thoughts before you begin talking.** This rule may be the most important, whether you're addressing one person or 1,000; whether you're speaking or writing. Know what you want to say — the point you want to make — before you start talking.

▶ **Get to the point.** Give your listeners the meat of your message up front, then elaborate with details.

▶ **Be yourself.** Don't think that to be an effective communicator you have to sound formal or use $10 words. Be real. Talk to your employees, colleagues and superiors with the same words and presentation style you always use. That doesn't mean you shouldn't build your vocabulary or improve your communication skills. Just don't act as if you're on a stage when talking with others. Letting your personality shine through will add impact to your message.

▶ **Be vivid.** Use images and symbols to bring your communication to life.

▶ **Be sensitive to the people with whom you communicate.** Pay attention to people's reactions to your messages, and respond accordingly. If people get upset by something you've said, ask them talk about their feelings.

▶ **Try to see the world through your listeners' eyes.** Put yourself in the position of the people with whom you want to communicate. This method is effective for helping to align people's perceptions.

▶ **Be easy to communicate with.** Be open and approachable. Treat people with respect. Let them know that you consider their responses and inputs vital to improved understanding and, therefore, increased productivity.

Guideline #5: *Listen actively*

Studies indicate that people spend 45% of their time listening — or at least acting as if they're listening. Considering that figure, communicating effectively is not a one-sided event. It must involve at least two people who are exchanging messages. For the exchange to be complete, you have to make sure the person you're talking to understands your message, and you must also focus on understanding others' messages.

Active listening — hearing and understanding what someone is saying to us — is obviously vital to effective communication. Here are several tips for listening more effectively:

▶ **Make a decision to listen.** From the minute someone starts talking, commit yourself to hearing and understanding what that person is saying.

▶ **Be open.** Don't stop listening to what someone is saying because you disagree with it or you think the person is wrong. Listen to the whole story without judgment.

▶ **Concentrate on the speaker and what is being said.** Don't let distractions or interruptions cause your mind to wander. Pay attention to the speaker's words, movements and emotions. Focus on the message.

▶ **Conquer the temptation to interrupt**. Let others finish what they have to say. Jumping in every time a thought pops into your mind irritates the person talking and makes it impossible for you to hear the message.

▶ **Ask questions.** Asking questions enables you to clarify your understanding of what others are saying. It also shows them that you are listening and encourages them to continue.

▶ **Take notes on the speaker's main points**. You don't necessarily need a pen and piece of paper to take notes. Make a mental list of the person's main points. Review the points periodically. This technique is great for retaining the information you receive.

Guideline #6: *Use feedback*

Giving and receiving feedback is vital to keeping a team functioning at peak capacity. Through feedback, you can give your employees direction and ideas for improvement. And if you want to take full advantage of the power of feedback, invite your employees to give you feedback on your performance.

Feedback is most often associated with evaluation periods, which we'll discuss in depth in a later chapter. But, there's no law saying you can't give employees feedback on a routine basis. If you notice someone doing something right, let that person know. If you have an idea that might improve an employee's performance, share it.

Keep in touch with your employees, and keep open the lines of communication. Invite your employees to do the same with you.

Tell them that you want to know if they are having problems or if they have any suggestions for improving the team's productivity.

To be effective, feedback needs to be:

▶ **Consistent.** Comment on your employees' performances on a regular basis. Don't just pop in with a tidbit of feedback now and then. Make it a point to give your employees equal attention. Don't focus on one person's performance while all but ignoring another employee.

▶ **Specific.** Give details when offering feedback. Don't just say, "You're doing a good job." Say "You handled that customer complaint beautifully." The employee thus learns what specifically you regard as "doing a good job."

▶ **Descriptive.** Pinpoint exactly why you think the employee's actions deserved praise. For example, you could say, "You let the customer explain the problem, you reassured him that we are interested in his satisfaction, and you asked him what it would take to make him feel better about our business. That's great!"

▶ **Immediate.** To pack more power into your feedback, share it as soon as you notice the behavior you want to address. Bring it up while it's fresh in your mind and in your employee's mind.

▶ **Sensitive.** Sensitivity is especially important when your feedback is to correct or scold an employee. Never do anything to embarrass or humiliate employees. Pick the right time and place. If you're angry, cool off. Wait until you think the person will be most responsive to the feedback.

Guideline #7: *Be aware of the impact of body language*

Have you ever watched television with the sound turned off? If so, you could probably tell the mood and tone of the scene just by watching the actors. You didn't need to know what someone was saying to detect the anger being portrayed. Nor did you need to hear strained violins in the background to detect fear. The actors' expressions and movements communicated all this to you.

Your facial expressions and movements communicate just as clearly to the people watching and listening to you. As a matter of fact, as little as 7% of any given message relies on the spoken or written word. The rest comes from non-verbal messages. Studies show that our tone of voice conveys 38% of our message, while 55% of it comes through our facial expressions and body movements. That's 93% of our communication! So, if you want to communicate effectively, use your entire body.

Let your attitudes and feelings show through your movements. Communicate strength and confidence when you move by walking with determination — head held high, shoulders back, and chest out. Look people in the eye when you talk with them, and speak clearly and confidently.

You can make your employees feel comfortable talking with you by smiling often, relaxing, sitting back with arms and legs uncrossed, and nodding to encourage them to continue talking. You can also communicate interest by moving to the edge of your seat and leaning toward the person talking.

In addition to using body language to communicate feelings and ideas, reading other people's body language is also a major part of understanding them. Listen to more than people's words. "Listen" to their expressions, their voices, their movements.

For example, if someone is looking at you with knitted brows or a deadpan expression, the message may convey a lack of understanding or concern about something you are saying. Stiff posture, a flat voice or fidgety hands and feet communicate stress. Listen to what people's voices and bodies are telling you.

Your success as a supervisor is linked directly to your effectiveness as a communicator. Good communication skills are vital for building relationships, explaining to your employees the company's objectives and inspiring them to strive for peak performance in order to achieve those goals. Make a commitment to become a master communicator.

Key Points

▶ For a company to use its resources fully, individuals on all levels must have the skills and the freedom to share information and ideas openly.

▶ Internal and external barriers complicate the communication process.

(1) Internal barriers include:
— Differing perceptions among people trying to communicate.
— Expectations.
— Prejudices and preconceived notions.
— Selectivity.

— Preoccupation.
— Emotions and attitudes.

(**2**) External barriers include:
— Interruptions.
— Distractions.
— Environmental conditions.

▶ Following a few simple guidelines can improve your communication skills:

(**1**) Be aware of the impact your actions and attitudes have on the messages your employees, colleagues, superiors and customers receive from you.

(**2**) Understand the forms of communication at work within the business environment.

(**3**) Keep the lines of communication open on the organizational level by sharing information freely.

(**4**) Present your message in a way that builds understanding.

(**5**) Listen actively.

(**6**) Use feedback to keep the two-way channels of communication open.

(**7**) Be aware of the impact of body language.

Self-Development Steps

(1) Improvement in any area usually begins by assessing your current skill level. Identify your major weaknesses and your strengths as a communicator.

(2) Design a plan for overcoming your weaknesses and developing your strengths.

(3) Develop a strategy for helping your employees become better communicators.

CHAPTER

5

COLONELS & CAPTAINS
Empowering Your Employees Through Delegation

"Our chief want in life is somebody who will make us do what we can."

— Ralph Waldo Emerson

Managers can come up with all kinds of excuses for not delegating tasks and responsibilities to their subordinates. Some may feel that their subordinates lack the experience and skills to do the job. Others may fear that the subordinate will make a mistake and the supervisor will get the blame. Here are some other common excuses:

▶ "My subordinates will think I'm giving them the job just because I don't want to do it."

▶ "I have to approve the final product, so why not handle it from the beginning?"

▶ "It'll take more time to show a subordinate how to do it than it will to do it myself."

▶ "My subordinates are as busy as I am. They don't have time for additional work."

▶ "This job is important. It demands my personal attention."

Those reasons make sense only in a superficial way. Yes, you're going to be held responsible for your subordinates' mistakes; that's part of the job description for a leader. It's all the more reason for you to impart to your subordinates the skills and knowledge they need if they're going to avoid mistakes. Yes, it may take you three hours to teach an employee to do a job you can perform in 30 minutes. But that three hours is a good investment, because if you've taught the employee well, the next time the job needs to be done the employee can do it all without your help.

Why Delegate?

There's only one problem with making excuses — **they don't get the work done.** And you can't do it all. If you could, would management have put you in charge of a group of employees? No, you would have been given the assignments to handle on your own.

A supervisor, by definition, is a delegator. If generals could do it all, there would be no need for colonels. If colonels could do it all, there would be no need for captains. Yet colonels and captains are not errand boys for generals. They are commanders, whose authority is respected by their subordinates.

As a supervisor, you are a commander. But like the person ahead of you in the chain of command, you must learn to delegate. If you're a colonel, you need to delegate to your captains.

You are not responsible for completing your team's assignments. Rather, you are expected to accomplish company objectives by directing and coordinating the efforts of your group. As a supervisor, your primary responsibility is to get your employees to reach their potential and to enable them to achieve peak performance. You must organize everyone's efforts under a master plan for reaching company objectives. To meet that challenge, you have to delegate.

Considering the complexity of that responsibility, it's not difficult to figure out why some supervisors cling to any excuse to avoid delegating. Delegating effectively isn't as simple as barking orders, then sitting back and waiting for positive results. To get maximum productivity, good supervisors realize that delegation is more than getting the work done quickly and efficiently. They strive to delegate work and responsibilities in a way that builds employees' strengths, helps them overcome their weaknesses and makes them valuable members of the company team.

Easy? No. Necessary? Yes.

Until you learn to delegate effectively, you and your team will not reach your full potential. Delegation is vital to effective management for several reasons:

Reason #1: *The power of synergy*

Synergy, a popular management concept, is the principle that the whole is greater than the sum of the individual parts. In other words, two people working together can produce greater results than two individuals working on the same task independently.

Here's a simplistic example: Let's say two individuals can lift 100 pounds apiece. That's 200 pounds between them. If they pool their strength, however, they can lift 300 pounds. That's synergy. The assembly line is a good example of synergy in action in business.

To capture the power of synergy, however, supervisors have to be able to coordinate their employees' work through effective delegation.

Reason #2: *Your productivity depends on delegating*

When you fail to delegate, you limit your own potential for development and achievement. No matter how talented, skilled, intelligent or energetic you are, you can't do everything. If you hope to meet even the minimum standards of your supervisory position, you have to learn to tap into your employees' abilities. The most effective way to do that is to delegate.

As you learn to delegate the responsibilities other employees can handle, you free yourself to focus on your management responsibilities. You don't exhaust your energies running around putting out fires; instead you train your employees to avoid starting them. Rather than getting bogged down in managing the day-to-day, minute-to-minute details of keeping your department going, you can concentrate on finding answers to the perennial management question, "How can we do what we do better and more profitably?"

Reason #3: *Delegation develops employees*

Effective delegation provides on-the-job training. Employees learn and grow within their positions when you give them tasks and responsibilities outside their normal routine of duties.

Let's say you've received a memo from a superior asking for copies of your past 12 monthly reports. Here's a perfect opportunity for training one of your employees on your department's computer. Someone else could do this task for you simply by pulling up the reports on the computer and printing them out.

The employee will have learned a skill, which increases his or her value, not to mention what it does for the person's self-image. Moreover, you now have an employee who can handle other computer-related tasks for you. That will give you more time to focus on the big picture of running your department.

Use delegation to challenge your employees to stretch beyond their comfort zones, and you will have more skilled and more enthusiastic employees. Most employees respond well to increased responsibility. They perceive it as a vote of confidence, a concrete symbol of your trust in them.

Delegation helps you focus areas for training. Through effective delegation, you can cultivate a well-trained, highly motivated staff.

Reason #4: *Peak performance from all*

You and your team don't function within a vacuum. What you do — your actions and accomplishments — have an impact on every aspect of your company. If any element within an organization is not performing up to par, the company is not performing up to par.

When you fail to delegate, the entire company suffers.

To take full advantage of all the resources at your disposal — yours, your employees' and the company's — and to produce the best results, effective delegation is crucial.

How To Delegate Effectively

Effective delegation is more than passing along orders or keeping people busy. When handled correctly, delegation is a well-planned strategy for optimizing the use of a team's resources. Achieving this objective doesn't happen by accident. It takes careful and thoughtful planning.

The following is a set of guidelines to help you plan and assign work in a way that achieves the team objectives and maximizes your potential and that of your employees.

Guideline #1: *Know when to delegate*

Unfortunately, you can't hand over every job to your employees. Some things you have to take care of yourself.

Delegating assignments, for example, must begin with you. You can't walk into the office in the morning and say to one of your employees, "Nancy, here's our work orders. Tell everybody what they're supposed to do this morning." You have to do that yourself.

Certainly, you can get assistance. An employee can do research, paper work or leg work for you, but, basically, you have to do the bulk of the work, and the responsibility is yours.

A major part of delegating successfully is being able to tell the difference between the responsibilities you need to keep for yourself and the jobs you can turn over to an employee.

Knowing when to delegate can be as simple as asking yourself the following questions:

▶ **What has to be done?** Compile a list of all the duties, tasks and chores for which you are responsible. You can do this on a daily, weekly or monthly basis. Once you've completed the list, ask yourself:

▶ **Do all these tasks need my personal attention?** When answering this question, consider several elements:

— The skills required to complete the job.

— The nature of the job. In other words, is it a confidential matter? Or are you the only one with the information needed to take the appropriate actions or to make the right decisions?

— Upper management's attitude toward the task. Are there some jobs it would prefer you handle yourself?

❱ **Can any of my employees handle these responsibilities?**
Knowing when to delegate depends on staying in touch with your
employees' capabilities.

❱ **Can I train any of my employees to complete these assignments, and is it worth the time it will take to train them?**

Understanding and answering that last question is vital to effective delegation. If a task is repetitive — one you find yourself
doing every week or month — then it pays to train a subordinate
to do it. The time invested in training will be repaid many times
over.

Guideline #2: *Match people to abilities and interests*

Let's say the computer program has been upgraded. An employee
will have to become familiar with the new software, then share the
information with everyone else in the department. If you have an
employee who's a whiz on the machine, why not assign the
responsibility to him or her?

That's the kind of delegation that increases productivity and
boosts morale. You are free to attend to other responsibilities, and
the employee builds his or her skills.

Delegating isn't just assigning those tasks you don't **want** to do.
If that's been your policy in the past, you probably haven't
received much cooperation from your employees. To ignite a
desire to learn and grow within their positions, give your employees responsibilities and duties that will challenge them and stimulate their interest in their work.

Be careful, however, not to overload employees with responsibilities they can't meet. Be familiar with their abilities. In other words, don't ask an employee who has absolutely no experience in accounting to take over your bookkeeping for the month. Build people's skills gradually through delegation. Don't throw them into foreign situations with little more than an order and a handshake. People get excited about new assignments and challenges only when they believe there is a chance they will perform successfully.

Early in my career, I took a job that should have provided me with some positive challenges. But my boss took the excitement out of it on the very first day.

This was a newly created job, so there were no previous standards to which I could compare what I was doing. I was introduced to the boss on that first day, and he told me: "I want you to do these three things."

He never came back to see what I was doing, and he never gave me any direction. He simply tossed the job in my lap and said, "Just do it." When I went back to him repeatedly to say "I need to talk to you; I don't understand what's going on; I need more guidelines," he would say, "You figure it out." My self-esteem was battered in that job, and I was miserable. I didn't stay there very long.

Giving employees duties they can't possibly complete will destroy their self-esteem and their morale. The best way to avoid this problem is to keep in touch with your employees' abilities. Talk with employees about their feelings when you give an assignment. This leads me to the third guideline for effective delegation:

Guideline #3: *Discuss assignments with employees*

"At its best, the delegation process is one of mutual consultation and agreement."[12]

In this age of employee participation in management and decision-making, that quote captures the essence of effective delegation. Employees don't want to be told what to do; they want to be involved in the plans for improving their performance and increasing their team's productivity.

What does this mean for you in your role as delegator? You need to be willing to talk with employees about their assignments.

When delegating a task or responsibility, spell out every detail of the assignment for employees. Always clarify these eight areas:

▶ **Responsibility.** Clearly outline assignments. For example, if you want one of your employees to handle some work for you while you're out of the office for a few days, tell that person exactly what you want done: answer the mail, file reports or whatever. Don't just say, "I'm leaving you in charge while I'm gone next week. Try to keep things in order for me."

▶ **Accountability.** Let employees know that they will be held accountable for completing the project or assignment. Talk to them about the consequences of failing to meet their responsibility.

▶ **Standards of performance.** Every job has certain standards. For example, if you ask a secretary to type a report for you, the minimum standards might include no typographical errors, neatness in presentation of material, and accuracy in facts and figures.

Make sure employees are familiar with the standards for all assignments.

▶ **Time schedule.** Deadlines are a vital part of business. Employees need to know what their deadlines are and why it is important to meet them.

▶ **Level of authority.** Give your employees the authority they need to complete the task you've assigned them. For example, if you've asked an employee to order supplies, make sure the people in the purchasing department will respond to the employee's requests. Urge employees to use their authority. If an employee has to come to you to get approval or endorsement for every move, that defeats the primary reasons for delegating — giving you more time and developing employee independence.

▶ **Schedule for follow-up meetings or reports.** Depending on the task or responsibility you're delegating, it's sometimes a good idea to establish up front a schedule for discussing progress or results on the assignment.

▶ **The assignment's relevance to the rest of the department and company.** People like to see how their actions or responsibilities fit into the larger picture within the department or company. Explain to employees how their work affects the department's productivity.

▶ **Employees' attitudes toward the responsibilities or tasks you are delegating.** When giving an assignment, make sure the employee is comfortable with it and perceives it as an opportunity, rather than as an unreasonable burden.

In addition to spelling out the details of these eight areas, make sure that employees understand what it means to accept an assignment. Let them know that you want them to assume personal responsibility for the task, to use the authority you've given them, and to produce positive results for the department, the company and themselves.

As you discuss an assignment with an employee, a written contract outlining the elements we've discussed can prevent confusion and misunderstandings. In the contract you can spell out exactly what is expected of the employee and your role, if any, in providing assistance.

Granted, written contracts are formal and often unnecessary, but in complicated or on-going assignments, they can simplify the delegation process. Getting assignments in writing can eliminate misperceptions and prevent needless mistakes.

Guideline #4: *See to it that employees have everything they need to complete an assignment*

When you give an assignment to an employee, you have certain responsibilities. Employees can only do as good a job as you enable them to do. To get top performance from employees:

▶ **Give them adequate authority.**

▶ **See to it that they have the right tools.**

▶ **Allow them access to human resources — other departments or personnel, if necessary — to complete the project.**

▶ **Give them the time and support they need to do a good job.**

Guideline #5: *When you delegate, let go*

For many supervisors, the most difficult aspect of delegation is giving up control. After all, ultimately it's your neck on the line. For delegation to serve its purpose, however, you can't hover over your employees, telling them every step to take to complete an assignment.

Give your employees freedom. When you're explaining the details of an assignment, focus on "what" needs to be accomplished. Let the employee develop the "how." And, once you've let go of the assignment, don't breathe down employees' necks, checking their every move or questioning their judgment on every decision. Not only should you let them try new techniques or methods; you also should encourage it. Innovation is a primary weapon in the battle to maintain a competitive edge in a crowded and complicated marketplace.

Keep in mind, however, that if you want your employees to be innovative, you have to be willing to let them make mistakes. Mistakes are a vital part of the learning process. If people aren't making mistakes, they are playing it safe, doing things the way they've always been done. It's probably a good idea to step in if you see an impending error that could do irreparable damage to your employee, your department or your company; but otherwise, give employees the right to be wrong.

I'm not suggesting that you abandon your employees once you give them an assignment. In addition to delegator, one of your roles as supervisor is mentor. Chances are that one of the reasons you're the supervisor is that you have more experience, more knowledge and more advanced skills than your employees. You can be a valuable resource for your employees as they undertake a delegated task.

My only warning is that you don't let employees hand their problems over to you. If they hit a snag, encourage them to design their own solutions. Listen to them and ask them thought provoking questions, but don't rush to their rescue. You can give them guidance without taking over their assigned tasks.

Remember: You delegate responsibilities to help your employees grow and to get the task off your worry list. Delegate, and let go.

Guideline #6: *Follow up on all assignments*

For delegation to be fully effective as a teaching tool, it's a good idea to follow up assignments with what you might call an assessment or review meeting with the employee. Once an employee has completed an assignment, or after someone has been managing a delegated responsibility for a while, have a meeting with that person to discuss performance and growth.

By examining an employee's performance, you can offer specific praise or detailed feedback on ways the worker can improve or enhance performance.

I have found it effective to start this type of meeting by asking employees about their feelings toward their assignments and their performance in meeting them. That way, they will be more open. With this approach, they don't feel the need to defend their performances. They will focus on the assignments and maybe even talk about ways they would do things differently the next time.

In addition to talking about the employee's point of view, share your perception and attitudes toward the completion of the assignment. You can offer praise for a job well done, and you might be able to give suggestions for improving or enhancing performance next time.

I want to stress that these follow-up meetings should be positive. Don't use them as an opportunity to point out everything the employee did wrong. Don't stroke your own ego by saying things like, "Well, I would have done it differently, but I guess your way does the job." Follow-up meetings can give you a perfect opportunity to build confidence and boost morale.

Guideline #7: *Accept responsibility*

Delegation has many benefits for supervisors, but it can't relieve you of the ultimate responsibility for accomplishing the work that has been assigned to your department. Turning over a task to an employee may free you from the burden of the work, but your shoulders must carry the ultimate responsibility. If something goes wrong, upper management will come to you for an explanation.

I have two rules when it comes to responsibility for the events in your department:

(1) Never direct blame onto an employee, even though that person may have been responsible for completing an assignment that went awry.

I'm not suggesting that, if something goes wrong, you cover for your employees. Upper management needs to know what is happening within your department, who is doing good work and who is not. But ultimately, it's up to you to make sure everyone is doing good work. You do this by cultivating your staff, and, when necessary, eliminating poor employees. That makes you ultimately responsible.

(2) Always share the credit for successes with your team.

A supervisor cannot accomplish anything worthwhile without a strong team. If you are praised for high output in your department, stress to upper management the role your team members played in your success. Pass along the praise to your team. Everyone likes to be complimented and recognized.

When The Shoe Is On The Other Foot

For supervisors, delegation is a two-way street. You may be a boss, but you also have a boss — who delegates to you. So, making the most of delegation to increase your company's productivity isn't only a matter of knowing how to give orders. You have to know how to take them.

Whether you're giving or taking orders, many of the same principles apply. They just look a little different when you're taking orders. Here are some pointers for making the most of delegating when the shoe is on the other foot:

Pointer #1: *Take an active role in the assignments*

Remember, the most effective delegation process is of "mutual consultation and agreement." Delegation works most effectively when everyone involved has a voice. Talk to your boss about the assignment. Discuss your ideas, opinions or misgivings. Ask for any specific guidance your manager might be able to provide. Take the time to clarify exactly what is expected of you. You may want a written contract, similar to the ones you would use with your own employees. Putting an assignment in writing can catch any misperceptions or miscommunications before they cause too much damage.

If you don't want a document as formal as a contract, you can always send a memo outlining your understanding of the task or responsibility to your superior. That way, you both will have a written record of your responsibility.

Pointer #2: *Realistic assignments*

Your superiors don't always know what you and your team are capable of. Sometimes they assign a task to you that you feel is impractical. For example, your boss might say to you, "We have a rush order for bird cages. Your department needs to increase production by 50% next week." If that's impossible, don't be afraid to speak up.

Accepting a responsibility at which you are destined to fail is not only threatening and demoralizing to you; it can also jeopardize your boss, who is ultimately responsible for your mistakes.

Certainly, you want assignments that stretch the abilities of you and your team. But don't set yourself up for failure. Be frank with superiors about your capabilities. If you feel insecure about an assignment, discuss your fears with your superior. He or she may be able to clarify details or to give you some direction so that you feel more confident. If nothing else, your boss can adjust or withdraw the assignment.

Remember, your primary goal is to do what is good for your department and for the company. You won't do anyone any good if you accept responsibilities you can't possibly meet.

Pointer #3: *Keep your superior informed*

Once you've accepted a job, stay in touch with your superior. I'm not suggesting that you pester your boss with details or with requests for help. But it is a good idea to keep your superior informed on your progress.

Give regular status reports on long-term projects, perhaps once a week or once a month. The reports don't have to be long and complicated — just detailed enough to let your superior know what's going on.

Let your boss know if you've hit any special snags. Tell him or her the cause of the problem, your plans for overcoming it, and any schedule or deadline adjustments the problem has caused.

Once you've completed an assignment, give your superior a full report. Sometimes it's even a good idea to request a meeting to discuss the assignment. You can review your performance or talk about ways it might have been completed more effectively.

Pointer #4: *Use assignments as self-development*

As I've said repeatedly, delegating is one of the most effective methods for developing employees — including you. To profit from experience when management gives you a new responsibility or task, commit yourself to peak performance. Aim for personal success, success for your superior and success for the company. Accept nothing less than the best from yourself.

Being on the receiving end of assignments can give you insight and ideas for working with your employees to develop workable assignments.

Key Points

▶ As a supervisor, your primary responsibility is to help your employees reach their potential and to enable them to achieve peak performance.

▶ Delegation is vital to effective supervisory management for several reasons:

(1) Delegation gives a work team the power of synergy.

(2) Your productivity and development as a supervisor depends on delegating effectively.

(3) Delegation is an effective method for developing employees.

(4) A company's profitability depends on peak performance from every individual and every department.

❫ Effective delegation is a well-planned strategy for getting the maximum use of a team's resources. These guidelines can help you design your delegation plan:

(1) Know when to delegate.

(2) Improve performance by matching people to assignments according to their abilities and interests.

(3) As you delegate tasks or responsibilities, discuss assignments with employees.

(4) See to it employees have everything they need to complete an assignment.

(5) When you delegate, let go.

(6) Follow up on all assignments.

(7) Accept the ultimate responsibility for all projects and assignments in your department or under your command.

❫ Delegation is a two-way street for supervisors. Here are some pointers for those times when you are the delegatee:

(1) Take an active role in designing the assignments you receive.

(2) Make sure the assignments you receive are realistic.

(3) Keep your superior informed.

(4) Accept assignments or additional responsibilities as opportunities to continue your self-development.

Self-Development Steps

(1) Analyze your patterns of delegation to determine if you are using delegation effectively. Ask yourself these questions:

— Am I spending more time doing the work that has to get done around here or managing the work?

— Could my team get better results if assignments were planned and distributed more effectively?

— Am I giving my employees the opportunity to develop to their full potential?

(2) Reviewing the guidelines offered in this chapter, list some actions you can take now that will improve your effectiveness as a delegator.

6

HUMPTY DUMPTY: PUTTING ALL THE PIECES TOGETHER AGAIN

Building Teamwork Into Your Team

"Standing alone as one person within an organization, you will have little impact on the world in which you exist. However, when several people work together, great things can be achieved." [13]

— Marion Hayes

People have lived and worked in groups since the beginning of mankind. To survive the hostile elements, our ancestors joined forces to hunt food, find shelter and defend themselves against enemies. Although the basic instinct to live and work in groups remains unchanged, the function and operation of groups has undergone radical transformations.

This is especially true in business. To meet the challenges facing us in the modern business arena, co-workers need to be more than a group. They must become a team. Humpty Dumpty cannot be reassembled by a collection of individuals acting randomly on

GROUP VS. TEAM [14]	
A collection of individuals.	A unit of people whose efforts are coordinated toward a preset result.
Members focus on individual goals.	Members focus on team goals.
Members work in environment of distrust; don't share goals, hence don't understand each other's roles.	Members understand how each other's actions mesh for common goals; trust one another; work in harmony.
Members seek training; see skill-development as just a necessary part of maintaining their jobs.	Members seek education; want to know how skills can best be developed and applied toward team goals.
Conflicts arise from internal competition.	Members solicit opposing viewpoints, seeking more effective methods to achieve team goals.
Encourages conformity.	Thrives on creativity.
Members see little connection between their aspirations and company goals.	Members have sense of ownership in projects; feel personal responsibility for projects' success.

their own. If you approach the task that way, the pieces won't fit and a lot of the eggshell fragments are going to be crushed underfoot.

Drawing a difference between groups and teams may seem like an exercise in semantics; the distinctions, however, are profound.

Changing groups into teams has been a slow process in the evolution of civilization. Even today, many supervisors treat their employees as a group. For this reason, they aren't eliciting the high levels of performance most teams are capable of.

To increase productivity, supervisors have to take the collection of individuals who work for them and meld their strengths, talents and ambitions into a single force.

The Makings Of A Strong Team

Successful teams share at least four vital ingredients:

(1) Objectives: Team members have to understand and accept their unit's common objectives.

(2) Roles: Team members have to understand their individual roles in reaching the unit's mission or objectives. They have to know what is expected of them and what they can expect of their team members and their supervisor.

(3) Guidelines: Team members have to understand the systems and methods the unit follows to accomplish its goals.

(4) Relationships: It's no secret that people who like one another can work together more effectively than people who can't get along. People who respect and trust one another are more likely to collaborate their efforts for a common cause.

All four of those ingredients are crucial to building an effective team. But there's no question in my mind that the way team members relate to one another on a personal and professional basis is the foundation of teamwork. Objectives, roles and guidelines are directional signals on the road to productivity; **relationships** provide the vehicle in which a team travels to its destination of maximum productivity. So building a team begins with building relationships.

As a supervisor, where do you start building relationships? You can create a strong team by developing several layers of interpersonal connections:

LAYER #1: *Your relationships with team members*

Dr. Wolf J. Rinke, human resource and management consultant, writes, "High performance teams are run by supervisors who spend a lot of time getting to know their personnel well."[15] He recommends that supervisors spend a minimum of 50% of their time with employees, getting to know them as employees and as people.

As I have said repeatedly throughout this book, your employees are your most valuable resource. Getting maximum performance from them is your primary goal. The most effective way to achieve that goal is to form strong relationships with your individual team members.

When I talk about building relationships with individual employees in my seminars, I sometimes hear supervisors say, "If I'm friends with my employees, I have no authority over them," and "If my employees think I want their friendship, they'll take advantage of me."

You do face a dilemma: How do you establish personal relationships with your employees, yet maintain a level of professionalism that allows you to be objective and to run your department effectively? You will find the answer to this question in the kinds of relationships you form.

Getting close to your employees doesn't mean that you focus on getting them to like you. That's not friendship. I'm talking about getting to know them, to understand them and to establish an openness with them.

Being friends with an employee does not mean you open yourself for abuse. Forming strong relationships with employees is the ideal method for handling employee concerns and problems.

For example, let's say an employee starts having problems. If you have a solid relationship with that person, you are more likely to say, "Jan, I've noticed a drop in your production over the last several weeks. Your past performance proves you can do better. Do you know what's causing the problem? I would like to help you work it out." The relationship provides a foundation for finding solutions, rather than slinging accusations.

Forming mature friendships with your employees improves the quality of work life for everyone involved. You don't have to play the bad guy to get people to produce. Employees don't have to deal with the hassles and frustrations of working for an uptight, uncommunicative supervisor.

The question now is: "How do you build solid relationships with employees?"

The foundation of any positive relationship is caring. You have to care genuinely for your employees, and they have to know you care. Talk to them about personal issues. Ask about their families and their interests or hobbies outside the company — anything that's important to them. Share a part of yourself with employees. Talk about your family and your interests. The supervisor who shows off pictures of his son communicates to his people: "I know there's more to each of us than the work we produce here."

When an employee is having a problem, whether it's at work or at home, offer your help and support. Sometimes just listening is enough. If an employee has a personal success, join in the celebration. Be genuinely excited for him or her.

Relating to employees on this level won't take up as much time as you may think. You can take breaks and lunches with your employees. You can have after-hours functions. The time spent cultivating relationships, whether it's on or off the clock, will be well worth it in terms of increased morale, better team spirit on the job and improved communication between you and the people you lead. Add all those benefits together and you end up with increased productivity.

So the first layer of building teamwork is to establish positive relationships with each of your employees.

LAYER #2: *Your relationship with your team as a whole*

In addition to building relationships with the individuals on your team, as a supervisor, you are also the leader of the team. That means you must relate to the group as a single, cohesive unit. You are their leader, their coach. It's up to you to provide the team direction, guidance and inspiration.

I won't elaborate on this point in great detail in this section. The principles and the how-to's I cover throughout the book focus on ways you can elicit peak performance through effective leadership.

LAYER #3: *Relationships with team members*

How well the members of a team get along with each other is obviously crucial to teamwork. As I said earlier, people who get along work more productively than people who simply tolerate one another.

Although you can't force people to get along, you can take steps to promote positive, productive relationships among your employees. The next section of this chapter gives more elaborate actions you can take to nurture the relationships among your employees.

For now, suffice it to say that a major part of your job as supervisor is to encourage trust and cooperation among your employees. Help them build relationships, work out differences and match their personal goals. Avoid doing things that can create problems. Holding contests that pit team member against team member, for example, doesn't always produce positive results. It often generates internal competition, which can result in counterproductive behavior.

LAYER #4: *Team relationships and others*

One word of caution concerning team spirit: Be careful not to promote detachment. Some teams become so wrapped up in their identity as a strong work unit, they stop seeing themselves as part of the company.

For example, marketing may see itself in competition with sales. A little healthy competition on this level can be fun, but don't let it get in the way of production. You don't want to let marketing sabotage sales' efforts to match or beat its performance.

As the team leader, you must stress the connection between your unit and the rest of the company. Talk about team goals in relation to corporate objectives. Teamwork needs to be company-wide, not just limited to individual departments or shifts.

Turning Your Group Into A Team

Supervisors have human instinct on their side when it comes to cultivating teamwork among their employees. People are instinctively drawn to groups. To get high productivity through teamwork, supervisors need only to build on that basic human drive.

Here are 9 tactics to help you turn a group of individuals into a team.

TACTIC #1: *Collaborative goal*

As I said earlier, objectives are a vital ingredient for building teamwork. Working for a common cause draws people together. It's really an amazing phenomenon. Even people who might otherwise be enemies become dedicated teammates when they focus on a mutual goal.

To use goals to fan the fires of teamwork, involve all members in goal-setting sessions. Certainly, some goals for your team will come pre-packaged, handed down from upper management. You and your team, however, will probably have the opportunity to set sub-goals for reaching an objective that upper management hands down. Solicit ideas, ask for feedback, and get commitments from team members.

Once goals have been established, it's vital that individuals understand their roles in reaching the objective. To build a sense of commitment to the team, be sure all employees have clear pictures of the impacts their actions will have on the team's success.

TACTIC #2: *Interdependence with team members*

As a supervisor, you know that your most valuable resource is your employees. But do your employees know that their most valuable resource is each other?

I've seen this situation time and again: Workers are willing to turn to their bosses for advice, guidance, solutions and assistance. Yet, many times they totally overlook the talents and skills of the people around them — their co-workers.

A vital part of teamwork is interdependence. Your employees need to perceive each other as helpmates, as resources who can answer questions, help solve problems and lend a helping a hand.

Urge your employees to turn to one another for help. One way you can encourage employees to use each other as resources is to make sure everyone knows each other and understands each other's strengths.

Think of an office manager who has a general description sheet on each of her employees. She might circulate these sheets so everyone would know about their co-workers' special skills and talents. That way, if someone had a question about the data-processing system in the office, that person could go straight to the employee who had the most information or experience on the system.

Enable and encourage your employees to lean on each other.

TACTIC #3: *Use challenges to strengthen bonds*

Nothing unifies the members of a team like a challenge. Walking onto the plant floor and saying, "I just got an order for 3,000 units by tomorrow afternoon" can trigger the powerful "if-we-pull-together-we-can-do-it" mood. Most people like a challenge, and if it's presented to them in a positive way, it can cause them to forget their differences and focus on doing what it takes to succeed.

Strengthen the ties among your employees by presenting work to them in terms of a challenge. Encourage them to organize and unite to meet the terms of the challenges.

TACTIC #4: *Use the buddy system*

People work better when they work together. This is true for several reasons. Primarily, people perform better when working with partners because they don't want to let their co-workers down. They know that if one person fails to do a good job, both will suffer.

Another reason people work better in pairs or teams is because it makes the work more interesting. If you have a tedious or unpleasant job to do, don't just put one person on it. Assign it to two or three people. Working with others takes the drudgery out of the dull jobs.

TACTIC #5: *Have fun together*

How much fun do your employees have? Do they seem glad to be working together? Having fun is an excellent means of building team spirit.

One idea for fun might be wacky work-place Olympics. You can design competitions based on the jobs your people do. Office Olympics might include changing typewriter flywheels or printer toner cartridges. An Olympic event in a shipping department might be transferring shipping popcorn from one box to another, and whoever spills the least is declared the winner. Be creative.

You don't have to spend all your time planning or conducting fun or off-the-wall events. Even one or two annual events can be enough to keep excitement pumping through the organization's veins.

People love a little friendly joking and camaraderie. Encourage it, and you'll be building teamwork. Of course, be careful not to let jokes or games break down relationships. Laughter should never be at the expense of an individual or group of people.

TACTIC #6: *Make the work environment enjoyable*

Who said work can't be fun? There are several things you can do to make your work place somewhere your employees like to be.

(1) Have group get-togethers on the premises occasionally. For example, have a team lunch once a month (or even more often, if you like). Or bring in doughnuts for the coffee break and invite people to visit with one another in the break room.

(2) Have a bulletin board for employee news. You can use the bulletin board for personal and business announcements about the people on your team. Post weddings, engagements, births, awards or whatever. People love to see their names on the board, and they like to know what's happening with the other people in their departments. Sharing this information builds a sense of "connectedness" among individuals.

(3) Hang humorous posters or calendars, if the work environment allows. This activity is especially effective if the items involve a subject or topic the people on your team can relate to.

TACTIC #7: *Create a tangible team symbol*

Symbols create a tangible sense of unity. If you doubt the power of symbols, scan the sports section of your newspaper, or check out the military post nearest you. Ask a Green Beret if symbols carry any team-building power. Or ask a local university football player.

For centuries, clans, groups, teams and clubs have sported symbols that communicate a sense of pride in membership.

You can identify team unity with trinkets as simple as caps, mugs or jackets. People like to feel they are part of a special group. A tangible symbol representing their membership builds pride in the group. When they feel this pride, they will cooperate in all efforts to maintain the group's elite or special status.

TACTIC #8: *Recognize accomplishments*

Most companies and departments reward individuals for outstanding accomplishments. But do you ever take special notice of the achievements your employees have accomplished as a team?

To build unity, reinforce the team as a whole, not just as a collection of skilled or outstanding workers. Emphasize the role teamwork plays in reaching goals.

TACTIC #9: *Conduct group training sessions*

Joint training and education build teamwork by giving people the opportunity to experiment and grow together. In a learning environment, people often let down their defenses and open up to one another as they attempt to master a new skill.

As you identify employees' training needs, divide people into groups for instruction, rather than teaching them individually. A positive side effect of this tactic is that you will also save time.

Although these techniques provide a powerful strategy for strengthening the bonds among your employees, their effectiveness as a team will depend on your leadership abilities. In addition to providing opportunities for team growth, strive to provide the kind of leadership that rallies your employees to peak performance.

Key Points

▶ To achieve maximum productivity, supervisors must take the collection of individuals who work for them and meld their strengths, talents and ambitions into a single force.

▶ Successful teams share four vital ingredients:
(1) Objectives.

(2) Roles.

(3) Guidelines.

(4) Relationships.

▶ Supervisors can build a strong team by cultivating several layers of interpersonal connections:
(1) Your relationships with individual team members.

(2) Your relationship with your team as a whole.

(3) The relationships among the members of your team.

(4) The relationship between your team and the rest of the company.

❯ Here are 9 tactics for increasing productivity through effective teamwork:

(1) Give the team a common cause.

(2) Cultivate interdependence among team members.

(3) Use challenges to strengthen bonds.

(4) Use the buddy system to increase job satisfaction and quality of work.

(5) Give your staff opportunities to have fun together.

(6) Make the work environment an enjoyable place to be.

(7) Give your team members a tangible symbol of their "teamness."

(8) Recognize team accomplishments in addition to rewarding individuals' efforts.

(9) Conduct group training sessions.

Self-Development Steps

(1) Do the members of your team understand the goals they share as a department? If not, develop a plan for setting goals and uniting your team for a common purpose.

(2) List some things you can do to improve your relationships with your individual employees.

(3) Plan a fun activity for your team. Get your employees involved in the planning stage. Ask them what they would like to do.

7

EGGSHELLS ON A ROLE
Motivating Your Team To Achieve Peak Performance

> *"The secret of happiness is not in doing what one likes, but in liking what one does."* [16]
>
> — James M. Barrie

When your assignment is to supervise the reassembling of Humpty Dumpty, there are two ways you can pose the challenge to your team members. You can tell them their job is to pick up eggshells. Or you can tell them their challenge is to reassemble an egg. The first approach tells them what to do. The second involves them in a project. The first approach gives them a task. The second challenges them to assume a role. The first approach demotivates. The second motivates. Much of our recent global economic history has revolved around the success of those societies in which people were challenged to assemble eggs and the failure of those in which people were told to pick up eggshells.

We will always remember the 1980s as an amazing period in world history. News of major social and economic reforms around the world competed for headlines daily.

But have you ever considered what forces were in action behind the headlines? How was a relatively small, densely populated and resource-poor country such as Japan able to move into a dominant position in world markets while a huge, resource-rich superpower such as the former Soviet Union, with 60 times the land area and 2.3 times the population, struggled to prevent the collapse of its economy?

I believe we can at least partially explain each country's economic status by examining its basic approach to people-management.

If you had gone to work in Japan in the early 1980s, here's a glimpse of what you might have experienced:

▶ You would have been given a dormitory room until you found housing.

▶ Your day at the office would have started with the company song.

▶ You would have been included in planning sessions for determining what is best for the company.

▶ You would have been assigned to a quality control circle, where you would have had a voice in production.

▶ Some days, you would have participated in formal ceremonies held to prevent monotony.

▶ You would have received membership in a social club, where you would have had the opportunity to take classes in arts, crafts and culture.

▶ You would have been rewarded for suggestions.

▶ Your supervisor would have known your name and have had basic background information on you.[17]

▶ Had you married, the company would have hosted the wedding and would have partially underwritten the cost for the ceremony.

▶ You would have been enrolled in continuous training.

▶ Senior middle management would have groomed you over a 10-year period in preparation for promotion.

▶ At the age of 55, you would have received a bonus equal to two years' pay, and would have worked shorter hours.[18]

The purpose of all these perks? They were part of a strategy to tap into employees' drive and ambitions — quite simply, to make them want to do good work.

Before the Soviet Union collapsed, you would have found a stark contrast to this caring environment. Workers in the communist system had very little incentive to work hard or to produce quality goods. Regardless of their output, they receive the same wages — what the state determines they need. Reports in the 1980s indicated that the pervasive attitude among pre-perestroika Soviet workers was that only fools invest more than minimal effort in their work.

The result: A military superpower that presented little or no competition in the global marketplace. In addition, the people of the country had to settle for poor-quality products and perpetual shortages. Today, this has caused severe problems for their people in trying to get back on their feet after their political system collapsed.

Obviously, this analysis is an oversimplification of a complicated issue. But the connection between production and motivation is clear when you examine the differences between the economic conditions of Japan and those of the Soviet Union before December of 1991.

Motivation is a key factor in production, regardless of the economic structure in which an organization is operating. In a free-enterprise system, such as that in the United States, worker motivation has a tremendous impact on a company's success.

Maintaining A Competitive Edge

You might be asking yourself, "So, where does the United States rank on the scale of worker motivation?" Let's put it this way: We could take a few lessons from the Japanese.

In spite of relatively good wages and pleasant working conditions (in most cases), a surprising number of workers in this country of capitalism and the American dream suffer from low morale. It has been estimated that 50% of employed Americans perform "just well enough not to get fired." And 75% could be significantly more effective. According to a government report, which analysts called "scary," American worker productivity increased only

0.9% in 1989, the worst showing since the 1980-81 recession.

Do these figures frighten you? They should, especially if they are reflective of your employees' attitudes. They should scare every American. Technological advances continue to compress the world into a global village. It's been a long time since American companies competed only with each other. In an increasingly complex marketplace, the only weapon effective against growing competition is high productivity.

Companies won't be able to maintain high levels of productivity, however, until America's business leaders learn to tap into their employees' desires and motivations. As a supervisor, you play a critical role in the United States' struggle to maintain a competitive edge in the marketplace. More than just about any other factor, the impact you as a leader have on your employees will determine their level of productivity. Your ability to accomplish your goals and the company's objectives is directly connected to your ability to inspire your employees to perform at maximum capacity.

Motivating Your Team

You can find volumes written on motivation and ways to motivate people. You could spend days studying all the theories on needs-satisfaction management and employee-incentive programs. And you would find that the point of all these philosophies and programs boils down to one basic truth — ***If you want to motivate your employees, give them what they want from their jobs.***

When I say that in my seminars, the typical response is, "What do they want? Our employees are paid fair wages. They work in a clean, safe environment. What more is there?"

A lot more. Good pay and good working conditions are basic. People expect at least that much from a job, and government regulations ensure that they get it. To build commitment in your employees, give them more than they expect. Give them what they want. And, what do people want?

Over the years, I have compiled a list of elements that most people want on the job.

ELEMENT #1: *Employees want effective leaders*

I've worked in all kinds of situations in my life, and I can tell you that nothing kills motivation like a supervisor or boss with no human relations skills or leadership ability.

The supervisor, just like any leader, sets the pace, the tone and the mood of the department. If you were to put the world's most motivated, committed team under an ineffective leader's supervision, that group's morale and productivity would begin to drop.

There's an old saying, "As the lead dog goes, so goes the pack." Even the most dedicated employees need leadership and guidance. If they don't get it, production will suffer. They may not stop trying. Their own personal integrity may not allow them to do less than their best work. But, a lack of leadership will unavoidably impair their productivity.

The most effective approach to building a motivated team is to commit yourself to becoming the kind of leader who inspires and enables others to achieve their best. I talked at length in the first section of this book on the importance of being more than a person who supervises; you need to be a person who leads. And, as I said in Chapter Two, leading others requires more than following a series of "leadership steps."

Unless you make the commitment to be the kind of person your employees will follow — someone they respect, trust and care about — the sharpest motivational "techniques" in the world won't stir your people to peak performance.

ELEMENT #2: *Employees want to think for themselves*

Some supervisors spell out every detail of an assignment for their employees. They walk in with a work order and start with, "This is what we have to do and here's how we're going to it." After giving step-by-step instructions, they ask, "Any questions?" After a one-second pause, they rush on with, "Good. Now get to work. I'll be back later to review your progress." You would think they were programming machines.

If you want your employees to get involved in what they are doing, let them use their minds. Don't go to them with plans for completing a project. Describe the assignment to them, and ask questions that will stimulate thought and input. For example, you could start by saying, "We have to switch over our record system to a new computer program." Then, ask questions such as:

▶ "Does anybody have any ideas on the best way to accomplish this task?"

▶ "What do you think it will take to make that plan work?"

▶ "Will that approach produce the results we want?"

❯ "Will the proposed action plan be consistent with our long-range objectives?"

Hold goal-setting sessions for your team. People who are involved in planning are more committed to the successful completion of a project.

This method also offers you a bonus: once your employees get used to thinking for themselves and designing solutions to the problems you bring them, they will become more independent. And you will have more time to invest in responsibilities other than planning assignments. You can guide your employees through the planning stages instead of spending time locked away in your office trying to plot every move yourself.

Give yourself a break and your employees a lift by tapping into their brainpower. Get them involved in the planning stages of assignments.

ELEMENT #3: *Fitting into the overall operation*

When you are responsible for only a single part of a company's production, it's easy to lose all sense of connection to organizational goals. For example, look at the people who work in the dye plant of a textile mill. They have a hand in only a part of a long process that results in clothing, linens and fabrics. Unless someone helps them draw the connection between their work and the quality of every item that leaves the mill, they may never realize the impact they have on the company's success.

To build your employees' commitment to corporate goals, make sure they understand the vital role they play in the company's overall operation. Show them how their work completes production.

Company tours are a good way to accomplish this objective. Tours allow people to see what the company is all about. They get an understanding of how their jobs fit into the big picture. This knowledge builds a sense of responsibility. Employees will recognize the effect their work has on other departments and on the company's ultimate goal of producing quality goods at the lowest cost.

Seeing the end results of their work also gives employees a feeling of accomplishment that is vital to feeling motivated. When we fail to see results from our work, we burn out and lose enthusiasm for our jobs.

In addition to company tours, you can keep your employees in touch with the rest of the company through videos, newsletters, meetings, retreats and events that involve everyone in the company. As a supervisor, you may feel that you're not in a position to coordinate company-wide events. You can, however, make suggestions to your managers and offer to organize a get-together now and then.

ELEMENT #4: *Make work interesting and challenging*

Show me the high achievers and super-performers on your team, and I'll show you employees who are feeling challenged by their work. Repetitive or boring tasks dull people's minds. It's hard to get excited about your work if it's putting you to sleep.

Assigning interesting work or giving employees a bit of variety, on the other hand, can be a strong motivational tool.

One way to keep work interesting is to cross-train your employees. Educate them on the different positions in your department.

That way, you can shift them from job to job so they don't get bored in one position.

Another method for enlivening work is to get your employees involved in training. When new people join the team, let veterans share their knowledge and skills with them. This tactic has several benefits. Not only does it break up the monotony for your workers; it also demonstrates your confidence in them. It builds teamwork by teaching employees to lean on each other as much as they lean on you, if not more so. And new employees get to know their co-workers as they learn their jobs.

Another way to build challenge into jobs is to give people the freedom to experiment and to solve problems on their own. Encourage your employees to ask themselves constantly: "How can we do better with what we are doing?" We can always improve the way we run a business or department, but only if we try new ideas. Let your team members know you respect their opinions and their expertise on the job.

Ask your employees for ideas that might make their work more interesting. Who knows better than they?

ELEMENT #5: *Employees want to be kept informed*

I've worked with some supervisors who live by the philosophy: "All my employees need to know is what their job is and how to do it. I'll let them know if that ever changes."

True, the company hired your employees to do a certain job, and as long as they have the information they need to get the job done, you've done an adequate job of informing them. But you will probably get no more than an adequate job from them in return.

Your employees want to feel like part of the company team. Think about it. Has upper management ever kept you in the dark on a certain topic or issue? How did it make you feel? As if you weren't part of the "inside" group? The incident probably didn't have a positive impact on your esteem, your morale, or your sense of commitment to the company.

One of the most discouraging phrases I hear from employees is, "They never tell me anything." The feeling that underlies that statement is a sense of being a non-person, just another part of the machinery that assembles the final product. Employees who feel this way don't have a sense of connection to the company or to their work.

Without a sense of connection, it is almost impossible for employees to feel committed to their work. It becomes just a job, a way to earn a paycheck. That attitude does not produce peak performance.

Keep employees informed. Let them know what is happening with the rest of the company. Tell employees your organization is expanding production before they read it in the local newspaper. Tell them as soon as it is feasible if the company is about to lay off part of the work force. That's not the kind of information a person wants to hear from a reporter on the evening news.

Keep your employees informed about what is happening within your department. Talk to your team if someone is being transferred or terminated. Don't let them discover it simply by the person's absence. Without violating the privacy of the employee in question, explain why you took the action you did. And, encourage employees to express their feelings.

Tell people when you are hiring new employees. Don't just introduce the new employee on the day he or she starts the job.

People are going to talk about the events that happen around them. You can control these discussions by giving employees the correct information. Or you can act as if nothing is happening and let the rumor mill churn out destructive misinformation.

When you share information with employees, you communicate respect. You communicate to them: "You are a part of this organization. I realize that what goes on here affects you, and you have a right to know what is happening. If you have any questions or comments, I'm interested in what you have to say."

ELEMENT #6: *Employees want to be heard*

One of the most common myths that hurts productivity is the idea that the communication process is a one-way street. That is, management passes information and instructions down to employees, but nothing ever needs be to transmitted from bottom to top.

The most successful companies treat communication as a two-way street that facilitates upward and downward communication. A steady flow of information and ideas circulates from management to employees and from employees to management. Leaders in these companies know that their employees can provide valuable insight into ways they can do their jobs more effectively. They also understand the basic human desire to be heard.

Listening to your employees has at least two benefits. First, you can learn from them. You get to see the working situation from their perspective. You know what's going on in their minds, and you can discover what turns them on.

Second, listening to employees acknowledges their value. It makes them feel that they are important, contributing members of the organization.

Make time in your schedule to listen to your employees. Solicit feedback from them. Ask them about their work and ways you might be able to help them increase productivity. Ask for their opinions. Sometimes it's even a good idea to hold what I call "gripe sessions."

By gripe session, I mean you allow a time when people can tell you what's on their minds. Ask whether anything is bothering them. Get information on what makes them unhappy or what they would like to see changed.

Once you get your employees to open up to you, it's important that you respond to their needs and suggestions. Don't just smile politely, nod your head and forget everything they've said by the time you get back to your office. Get involved in what they are saying.

A plant manager I once worked with learned this lesson the hard way. He was having difficulty communicating with the supervisors who worked under him. He thought the problem was with the supervisors, so I was called in to help them out.

I spent a lot of time working with the supervisors on the techniques of basic supervision. Then the plant manager was asked to come to one of the classes. The class turned into a gripe session, with the supervisors filling him in on the changes they wanted to see implemented.

"I hear what you're saying," said the plant manager.

But two years later, he still had not responded. Company management did respond. That plant manager was dismissed, and it was the workers themselves who brought it about, because he refused to listen to their needs.

When subordinates air their complaints to you, ask them for details. To clarify understanding, feed back to them what you hear them say. If employees complain to you about a problem, ask them questions that will lead them to discover a solution on their own. Work together to design a plan of action to overcome problems or complaints. Let employees know what you plan to do in response to their comments or suggestions.

For example, let's say an employee tells you, "I can't meet my production quota if the people in the assembly department don't speed up." You can respond by clarifying the problem, then saying, for example, "I'll set up a meeting with Higgins in assembly and find out why they seem to be having trouble keeping up with our team."

Let employees know that you have heard what they are saying, that you value their input, and are committed to enabling them to achieve peak performance.

ELEMENT #7: *Employees demand respect*

If you don't give employees respect, you will usually end up with an apathetic team that puts in the hours but not the dedication needed for a department to achieve peak performance.

People's actions reflect their self-image. If you treat your employees like losers, they will act like losers. If you treat them like winners, they will give you winning performances.

Praise, recognition and reward are effective for building self-esteem and a willingness to get involved in the job. I suggest both formal and informal recognition for employees who do good work. Rewards, incentives and bonuses are important to employees because they represent concrete, tangible credit for work well done. We all love a pat on the back now and then. It's a simple gesture that says, "I notice your work and appreciate your dedication. I value you as an employee and as a person."

Employees who feel appreciated are more committed to their work, to you and to the company.

ELEMENT #8: *Represent employees interests*

If you remember, I said at the beginning of this book that the position of supervisor is one of the most challenging in a business. You are the connection between upper management and the people you supervise. One of the most difficult aspects of that position is that you have to maintain a balance between company demands and employee needs.

Obviously, your primary responsibility is to the company, just as it is for every employee. Maintaining a strong organization is the only way you can provide job security for the people who work for you. That fact, however, doesn't mean that you completely ignore or trample on your employees' needs.

Taking care of your employees, building in them a sense of belonging and of importance, is a part of fulfilling your responsibility to the company. Building strong, committed employees is your job. To develop a sense of commitment in your employees, you must represent their interests to management.

You, better than anyone else, understand your employees, their needs and the work from their perspective. You are responsible for explaining that perspective to your superiors. If you believe a management directive is harmful to your employees and their morale, you need to take a stand for your team. Work for solutions and compromises that protect their needs.

ELEMENT #9: *Respect individuals*

A big problem many business leaders have with motivating employees is that they assume everyone wants the same things. These same leaders assume that employees are motivated by the same forces that motivate them to work hard and achieve.

Ah, but were it so easy!

Consider a survey of thousands of employees in various industries.[19] Researchers asked employees to list 10 items in order of importance to them. Another part of the survey instructed supervisors to rank the items in what they thought to be the order of importance to their employees. Here are the results:

Survey of Employees

Employee Ranking	Item	Supervisor Ranking
1	Recognition for good work	8
2	Feeling of being "in on things"	10
3	Understanding & help on personal problems	9
4	Job security	2
5	Good wages	1
6	Challenging work	5
7	Promotion and growth in company	3
8	Company loyalty to employees	6
9	Satisfactory working conditions	4
10	Tactful disciplining	7

These figures opened some eyes. People don't necessarily want what we think they want, or what we would want if we were in their position. To tap into another person's motivational drives, we must seek to understand what that individual wants.

The best way to do that is to get to know each of your employees individually, as I discussed in an earlier chapter. Understanding an employee as a person can give you great insight into him or her as a worker.

For example, let's say you have an employee who comes in right on time every day and leaves right at quitting time. He doesn't work less than eight hours a day, and he doesn't work more. If you get to know this person, you might learn that he has family responsibilities that limit the number of hours he can work. This information can be useful if you need him to work overtime for you. Compensatory time off might be a stronger incentive than overtime pay for him.

You might have another employee with strong ambitions to grow in the company. You can reward that person with increasing responsibilities and continuing education opportunities both on and off the job.

Certainly, everyone wants the basics — good salary, good working conditions and fair treatment. If you want to maximize every employees' potentials, however, learn to respond to their individual needs and drives.

The most effective way to keep your team motivated is to use your employees to their fullest potential in a way that gives meaning to their work, and to reward them for that commitment.

Key Points

▶ Motivation is a key factor in production, regardless of the economic structure in which an organization is operating. In a free-enterprise system, such as in the United States, worker motivation has a tremendous impact on a company's success.

▶ To build commitment in your employees, give them more than they expect. Give them what they want. Here is a list of elements that most people want on the job:

(1) To work for effective leaders.

(2) To be allowed to think for themselves.

(3) To know how their work fits into the overall operation and success of their company.

(4) Interesting and challenging work.

(5) To be informed.

(6) To be heard.

(7) Respect.

(8) Supervisors who will represent their interests.

(9) To be treated as individuals.

▶ Using your employees to their fullest potential in a way that gives meaning to their work and rewarding them for that commitment is the most effective way to keep your team motivated.

Self-Development Steps

(1) Motivating your employees for peak performance depends on responding to employees' individual needs and wants. Develop a strategy for getting to know your employees and identifying ways to tap into their energy and commitment.

(2) Based on ideas suggested in this chapter, list any areas in which you can make improvements that would result in higher morale among your employees.

8

ROSES AND THORNS: TELLING IT THE WAY IT IS
Evaluating Employee Performance

"Criticism is properly the rod of divination: a hazel switch for the discovery of buried treasure, not a birch twig for the castigation of offenders."

— Arthur Symons

Arthur Symons wrote about literary criticism, but the analogy works as well for performance evaluations in the work place. You may find it hard to believe, but the evaluation process was not originally designed as a torture device for employees and their managers. Legend has it that somewhere someone came up with the idea that if bosses and employees could talk openly, reviewing the employee's performance and the supervisor's job as manager, they could work together to ensure that the team was producing at full capacity and everyone would live happily ever after.

This view may be a bit optimistic, but I believe the concept of evaluation as a way to build understanding between managers and their employees, and, therefore, enhance performance, is still valid today. You as a supervisor can draw many benefits from conducting formal evaluations.

As you go about the evaluation process, remember that there are roses and thorns in every performance. The rose provides the aroma of achievement; the bloom of success. But the pleasure of the blossom can be punctured quickly and painfully by the stab of the thorn. The wise supervisor will provide praise for the rose, but will be alert for thorns that need to be eliminated, or at least avoided.

BENEFIT #1: The process of effectively evaluating employees forces you to focus on your workers as individuals.

Effective evaluations don't begin the day you sit down with an evaluation form and start marking columns under an employee's name. The process is ongoing.

For employee evaluations to be valid, you have to record information about employees on a continuing basis. If an employee turns in a top-notch performance, you need to make note of the rose in that person's file. If you notice an attitude problem developing, that thorn needs to be identified and logged into the record at that time. That way, when the six-month or one-year review period rolls around, you have records that reflect employees' long term performance histories, and not just the activity of the last week or two before evaluation interviews are scheduled to begin.

This process, therefore, forces you to pay attention to your employees on a day-to-day basis. You have to make an effort to evaluate their individual performances almost daily, or least weekly or monthly. I know it's tempting to hand out assignments, give your employees free reign, then close your door so you can get some work done. That way, the only time you have to look up is when something starts to go wrong. That's not an effective method, however, for getting to know the people who work for you or for enabling them to achieve maximum productivity.

To help employees reach their potential as individuals and as a team, you have to know them. You can't routinely review employees' performances without learning about individuals and how they work together best.

Formal evaluations facilitate the process of becoming more familiar with the people on your team and discovering ways you can help them increase their productivity.

BENEFIT #2: Formal appraisal interviews give supervisors and their employees an opportunity to discuss important issues in depth.

In a busy company, you don't have many chances to talk with employees on a one-on-one basis. Even if you have an open-door policy inviting employees to come to you with ideas, suggestions, problems or complaints, the business of getting work done usually gets in the way of conversations and rap sessions. That's great if your team is so productive its members don't have a lot of time for schmoozing.

It's important, however, for you to stay in touch with the individuals on your team. The only way to maintain relationships with your employees is to talk with them. You can talk about their attitudes and feelings, and you can share with them what's going on inside of your head. I'm not saying you have to get "touchy-feely," but it helps to open up with your employees occasionally.

During appraisal interviews, you and your employees have the time to delve into issues concerning you and them. An employee may be having problems mastering a certain aspect of the job. Finding a solution may require some probing to discover the root of the problem. Without a formal interview, the employee may never approach you for help, or you may never set aside enough time to give the problem adequate attention.

Scheduled evaluation interviews provide a vital link between you and your employees.

BENEFIT #3: By conducting effective evaluations, you communicate your commitment to developing your employees to their fullest potential.

Formal evaluations are concrete actions that let employees know that you are sincerely interested in them and in enabling them to do the best job possible. Most people want to do good jobs. They respond positively when they sense that you want to help them to accomplish this objective.

Letting people know you are committed to helping them develop cultivates their sense of self-worth. You are, in essence, saying, "You are worth the investment needed to help you do your best."

Constructive evaluations give employees direction and encouragement, and that's a vital element in a broad strategy for building employees' sense of importance. Letting employees know that they can make a difference builds their commitment to achieve peak performance.

BENEFIT #4: Formal evaluations provide objective records necessary for making critical personnel decisions.

As supervisor, you play a major role in deciding who gets raises, who gets promoted and who gets disciplined or terminated. Trying to make decisions objectively can be one of the most difficult challenges you face.

When it comes to making decisions about people, it's impossible to be completely objective. The way you feel about a person is inherently subjective. You might not have positive feelings toward an employee because your personalities clash. Let's say the person produces good work, has a good attitude and has potential to grow within a position. But you just don't like him or her. Those feelings can affect your judgment. You may spot the thorns and overlook the roses.

On the other hand, you may have an employee who is a pleasure to be around. This person is always upbeat, always cooperative. Yet, he or she doesn't have adequate skills for the position and seems incapable of development. You wouldn't be the only supervisor who would be tempted to give that person higher marks than the employee in the first example. Why? Simply because you like the individual. You're so enamored with the roses that you overlook the thorns. I've seen it happen. All of us occasionally let unrelated characteristics or features distract us from the issues.

Another factor affecting the objectivity of personnel decisions is that we often base our judgments on employees' most recent performance histories. Let's say, for example, that an employee, who normally turns in a no-more-than-adequate performance, produces fantastic results on a project right before raises are decided. You might be tempted to give him or her a generous pay increase, based on that single incident.

There are no simple answers for removing subjectivity from personnel decisions. Supervisors are only human. We can, however, reduce subjectivity to a minimum by following a formal evaluation system that tracks employee conduct and performance routinely and objectively over a period of time. By following formal evaluation procedures, which you and your employees understand, you judge all employees on the same criteria, and you have a record of their overall performance, not just their latest accomplishments.

Not only are your decisions more equitable under a formal system, but also you have written records for justifying your decisions, and that factor can be crucial in certain personnel matters.

I've worked for companies that didn't have formal evaluation systems, and I've worked for companies that did. I can tell you this: When done correctly — and that is the key — evaluations can produce rich rewards in the form of high morale, enhanced teamwork and increased productivity.

If that information alone is not enough to convince you that evaluations are a part of any successful supervisory management strategy, let me add that you can make evaluations a positive experience for yourself and your employees. They don't have to be painful or tedious. It all depends on your attitude and your approach to evaluations. Once you learn to conduct constructive evaluations, you can unleash your team's potential for achievement.

Evaluating For Growth

I believe one reason people react so negatively to evaluations is that they've had few positive experiences with them.

Some supervisors use the evaluation as a tool to manipulate employees. They reason, "If I give good marks, my employees will start to slack off. I'd better give everyone marks just below their actual performance levels. That way, they'll try harder."

Other supervisors perceive evaluations as a necessary evil. To them, it's just an exercise — one more bit of paperwork they want out of the way. So they invest as little time as possible in evaluations, giving all employees "average" marks across the board. Poor work is graded the same as great performances.

Both these approaches usually result in demoralized employees who see no connection between their output and the rewards or recognition they receive.

As the supervisor, maybe you've had some negative experiences when you tried to go over an evaluation with an employee. Some people walk into their interviews with defenses up. One word of criticism from you — even constructive guidance — and they yell harassment. Their attitudes deteriorate right before your eyes, and pretty soon you're looking for a replacement.

A second reason many people respond negatively to evaluations: Evaluations are steeped in emotion. For most of us, our work identifies who we are. When you meet new people, what's one of the first questions they ask you? "What do you do?" We are what we do. Our identity and our sense of purpose in life are wrapped up in our jobs. You start poking holes in a person's job performance and you are, in essence, poking holes in that person. So, it's understandable that people react emotionally to judgments about their work.

Fortunately, the bad attitudes people have toward evaluations and the fears they bring with them into the appraisal interview are not a necessary part of the evaluation process. When approached correctly, evaluations can be a positive experience, a management tool that helps employees grow and maximizes production.

Educate Your Employees On Your Evaluation System

Effective evaluations begin in your mind and in the minds of your employees. If you want to build a constructive evaluation system, you and your employees must perceive the process as an opportunity for growth.

Effective evaluations are founded on understanding. To build a positive attitude toward evaluations, educate your employees.

First, make sure employees understand your attitude toward evaluations. They need to know that you use evaluations as a way to keep in touch with their needs and as a way to maximize the team's performance. Plant a positive attitude in their minds toward the evaluation process.

Secondly, educate your employees on exactly how your system works. Explain in detail in what areas they will be evaluated. Most employers, for instance, rate employees on factors such as job skills and knowledge, attitude and punctuality. In addition, let employees know which areas carry the most impact. Job skills and knowledge, for instance, are usually top priorities. Assigning one area priority doesn't mean the other qualities are unimportant. It just allows employees to focus their attention on developing in the more crucial areas. Employees must understand what's expected of them at all times.

Explain to them how the evaluations will be used. Tell them what kind of impact their evaluations will have on raises and promotions.

Let employees know how often you will conduct evaluation interviews, and describe for them the interview format. The more employees know about what to expect, the more comfortable they will feel with the entire process.

Third, describe the role you play in enabling workers to reach peak performance. As their supervisor, you have a tremendous impact on your employees' ability to reach their objectives. Let them know that you acknowledge and accept this responsibility and that they have every right to evaluate your performance on this level.

How To Conduct An Effective Appraisal Interview

The rubber meets the road in the appraisal interview. All your record keeping, all your attempts to stay in touch with employees, and all your promises to use evaluations constructively will count for nothing unless you conduct the interview correctly.

Here are several pointers that can make your evaluations more productive:

POINTER #1: *Emphasize the positive*

If an employee is giving a consistently superior performance, don't hesitate to ring bells, blow whistles and praise the performance long and loudly. In my opinion, you can never be too positive when reviewing a good employee's performance. Contrary to some management theories, most people respond to praise by working harder, not by slacking off.

Unfortunately, most employees don't fall into the "super performer" category. Most of them can use some guidance and improvement. But that doesn't mean you can't be positive.

Let's say, for example, you have an employee who seems to be having trouble mastering a new job skill required for his position. You might approach this dilemma positively by saying, "Joe, I appreciate that you've been concentrating on learning how to use the new equipment in the processing room. How I can help?"

That approach focuses on the issue, not on Joe as an employee. It begins with a positive statement, and is directed toward finding a solution, rather than toward blaming Joe for not learning quickly enough. Because he doesn't have to fend off an attack, Joe will be more open to suggestions and guidance.

The goal in effective evaluation interviews is to open dialogue between you and your employees, which can lead to better understanding. That way, you can work together to increase productivity.

To establish free-flowing dialogue with others, you must emphasize the positive. Talk in terms of improvement and potential, rather than failure and blame.

It's also important to let employees know well ahead of time when you will hold the appraisal interview. Employees will feel threatened if you spring an unannounced evaluation interview on them. Even a positive review loses some of its impact if an employee feels ambushed.

POINTER #2: *Focus on objectives*

The purpose of evaluations, like most of your management responsibilities, is to enable employees to meet objectives, which include company goals, team goals and individual career goals. When you're reviewing an employee's evaluation record, talk in terms of meeting those objectives.

For example, you might say to a worker, "Ellen, I've been impressed with your commitment. You've been willing to work overtime at least one week a month for the past six months. That dedication has enabled this department to meet its quotas and then some. Your participation in this team effort has been crucial to meeting our company's commitments to our customers. This is the kind of dedication upper management looks for in supervisory prospects."

That way, you draw a connection between performance and the company's goals, which are directly related to the employee's personal goals.

POINTER #3: *Be honest and candid*

Only accurate evaluations can have a positive and significant impact. Always be completely honest with your employees. Don't beat around the bush, and don't disguise criticism in so many layers of sugar that employees miss your message. Always be frank with your employees.

If you feel employees are working at maximum capacity, tell them so. Then you might explore ways to help them increase their production through continuing education or development. Always focus on improvement. No matter how good we get, we can always get better.

If you believe an employee seems to be unable or unwilling to give the best, explain your perception to the individual. Until you get to the truth, you won't be able to uncover problems. Try to determine what might be impairing an employee's performance. And remember: Approach the problem constructively. Focus on solutions, not on blame.

Candor communicates respect. By giving the facts as you see them, you say to employees, "I know you are professional enough that we can talk about these problems and work together to form a solution."

POINTER #4: *Professional and mature interviews*

First, always treat the employee with respect. Always remember that you are dealing with another person — someone with feelings, fears and a need to be validated.

Whether you're handing out accolades or constructive criticism, treat your employees like professionals. Don't patronize them, but don't run roughshod over their feelings, either.

Second, avoid getting into arguments over appraisals. An employee might respond to your evaluation by saying, "That's not true. How can you say I don't work hard enough? I work my butt off." Don't argue about it. Try to understand the individual. You might say, "Well, I've just given you my perception of your work. Tell me how you feel about it." Don't get into shouting matches or a tug-of-wills. **Always focus on building your employees' skills, not on proving to them that you are right and they are wrong.**

Third, when meeting with an employee, discuss only that individual's performance. Never talk to your employees about co-workers. If you have to get something off your chest, talk to a peer or to a superior. Talking to one employee about another erodes their trust in you. While you are talking, they are thinking, "So, what are you telling everyone else about me?" That's a morale killer.

Fourth, close the interview only after you're certain you and the employee understand one another: You both agree on the evaluation, you've defined any performance problems and settled on solutions, and you've reinforced what the employee is doing right. Always try to build understanding with employees in each interview.

Although you don't want to condemn yourself to stiff and uncomfortable evaluation sessions that employees dread, it's important to keep all interviews on a professional level.

POINTER #5: *Invite and facilitate a two-way exchange*

How do you picture an evaluation interview in action? Do you see the supervisor going down a list, noting how an employee ranks in the areas being reviewed? That may be the traditional image, but it's not an effective approach. Evaluation interviews that produce results get the employee involved in the process.

Ask employees to review their own performances. Some supervisors give copies of the form they use to their employees and ask them to fill them out. They use both the evaluation sheets to discuss the employee's performance.

Encourage employees to evaluate your effectiveness as a supervisor. As I said earlier, you are responsible for enabling your employees to achieve peak performance. It's only fair — and wise — that you give them the opportunity to share with you their opinion of how well you meet that responsibility. When I say it's wise, I mean that sometimes we don't have the most accurate picture of ourselves in our minds. In much the manner that your appraisals can help employees identify their weaknesses, your employees can help you see yours. The most effective evaluation interviews are two-way streets.

In addition to evaluating performances — theirs and yours — ask employees for input on the organization. Do they have any suggestions or ideas? Can they suggest any company or department changes that might help them do better jobs?

Evaluation interviews are a perfect time for picking your employees' brains.

POINTER #6: *Action plans*

The purpose of evaluations is to improve performance. To ensure that your appraisals are more than exercises in futility, close evaluation interviews with a plan of action.

An effective way to wrap up evaluation interviews is first to summarize the points covered in the meeting. Make sure you and the employee share the same perceptions of the results of the meeting. As you summarize the meeting's main points, clarify any agreements.

If necessary, arrange a follow-up meeting. Sometimes in an evaluation interview, you will set up a schedule for improvement or change. Go ahead and establish a time to meet and review the employee's progress.

For evaluation interviews to have the most impact, never leave details hanging. Always discuss the future with employees and review plans they have for adjusting or improving their performance.

Handling Personnel Problems

Although I have emphasized the importance of approaching evaluations and appraisal interviews positively, I recognize that many times supervisors must deal with serious problems involving individual employees. Undisciplined behavior or special employee problems, such as substance abuse, which result in poor performance, can have a devastating effect on the productivity of your work unit. Don't let them go without comment or action.

As a supervisor, you have to impose certain standards of behavior and performance on employees. A company's survival depends on it. That doesn't mean, however, that your only option is to attack or eliminate "problem" employees. There is a more constructive approach — **performance counseling.**

Through performance counseling, you focus on identifying the causes of employees' problems, and work to eliminate them. Performance counseling replaces the conventional concept of discipline.

In the past, discipline has usually been a negative aspect of supervising employees. If an employee failed to meet a standard or exhibited unacceptable behavior, the supervisor would react with what amounted to a form of punishment. The punishment might involve anything from revoking privileges to suspending or terminating the employee. There is still a place in today's business environment for revoking privileges and suspending employees, temporarily or permanently. But smart supervisors use these tactics for different reasons in performance counseling.

Always approach performance counseling from a positive point of view. Remember, your goal as a supervisor is to increase and improve your employees' production. It's not your job to punish employees or to teach them a lesson if they step out of line. When you approach an employee about a problem that's interfering with their work, your primary goals should be to look for a solution that will benefit the employee and the company.

To get the most effective results when trying to help employees work through their problems, I suggest the following tips:

TIP #1: *Have all the facts*

First of all, know the problem. Exactly what is the employee doing or failing to do that is interfering with that person's work or the work of other employees? Be sure you have an accurate perception of the issue before you confront an employee. Have you seen the employee committing the offense? What evidence do you have of a problem? Don't jump to conclusions, and don't act on hearsay. As you define the problem, try to determine the cause or the reason for the situation and what it would take to solve it.

Secondly, review the company's policy on the issue. Let's say you have an employee who seems incapable of starting work on time. Where does the company stand on this issue? Does it dock workers' pay? Does it allow workers to make up lost time on lunch hours? Find out what is standard procedure for the company before you start struggling with how to handle the situation.

Third, know the employee involved. Is this person a habitual troublemaker or goof-off? Does the problem stem from a one-time occurrence, or is it a regular event? And how is the behavior in question affecting the employee's performance and the performance of co-workers? How serious is the offense in relation to the employee's overall performance?

TIP #2: *Make sure your employees have all the facts*

Employees need to be familiar with company policies from the first day on the job or as new policies are introduced. Let them know what is expected of them in terms of conduct and production.

In addition, inform employees about the consequences of failing to follow company policies or to meet standards for performance or behavior. For example, most companies have a multi-layered discipline system:

❱ Verbal, non-recorded warning.

❱ Written warning that becomes a part of an employee's permanent record.

❱ Suspension from work.

❱ Discharge.

Employees have the right to know what their actions will cost them.

TIP #3: *Discuss problems when you notice them*

Most problems will not disappear simply because you ignore them. Many difficult situations involving people only grow with time. So as soon as you can, let employees know that you recognize there is a problem.

Problems that occur without comment are likely to continue. The employee may not be aware that the behavior is causing a problem. Or the individual may think, "Well, if no one is going to tell me to stop doing this, it must not be a big deal."

Allowing one employee to break the rules also sends a negative message to the rest of your staff. You are in essence telling them that you don't enforce the rules and they can do as they please. Employees who are committed to doing a good job will resent this attitude, especially if it hurts the quality of their work. Employees who are less than totally responsible will follow the example set by the employee who started the problem.

Don't let problems grow. Address them as soon as you notice them.

TIP #4: *Be frank and open*

Honesty and candor are vital for effective performance counseling. The best approach is simply to state your perception of the problem and explain to the employee exactly why it is a problem.

For example, you might say, "Chris, I've noticed that the quality of your work has been slipping for the past couple of weeks. People in your work group are complaining because it's affecting the quality and speed at which they can produce. Can we together work out a solution?"

Be positive, but be honest and firm.

TIP #5: *Focus on the behavior or issue, not the employee*

Instead of saying, "You are disrupting the work flow in this department," you might say, "Your behavior is disrupting the work flow in this department." That way, the employee is less likely to feel that you are making a personal attack and will focus on the behavior, not on making a defense before you.

When you focus on issues, you are free to concentrate on finding solutions to the behavior problems instead of on trying to change an individual, which is virtually impossible.

Look for constructive solutions or ways to modify behavior. You might start the process by saying, "This behavior is causing a problem. Do you have any suggestions for ways to change it or prevent it from happening again?" Let employees design solutions to their problems as much as possible. Have them take possession of the idea. That way, they will be more likely to live up to it.

TIP #6: *Be consistent*

If you want your employees to respect you and to feel committed to the team, demand the same level of performance and the same standards of behavior from all of them. And when someone does step out of line, respond to all violations the same. Playing favorites breaks down team spirit and severely cripples your effectiveness as a supervisor.

TIP #7: *Keep your superior informed*

Depending on the seriousness of the problem, it's a good idea to keep your manager informed about any personnel difficulties. Your superior needs to know what's going on with the people under you. Moreover, they might be able to provide guidance on how to handle problems most effectively.

TIP #8: *Handle special employee problems with care*

When you hire a person, you don't just hire the brains and brawn needed to get the job done. You hire an entire package that comes with emotions, outside interests and problems. We all have personal problems on occasion that distract us from our work. Some difficulties are more distracting than others and need to be addressed.

Alcoholism, drug abuse and family crises are three realities that cost businesses billions of dollars every year in lost productivity. They are realities that you will probably face as a supervisor. Part of leading in the contemporary business world is helping employees improve their performances by helping them cope with personal problems.

We could fill an entire volume with ways to help employees maintain their performances while working through these problems. The issue is complex, and companies have different policies and regulations concerning private personnel matters. So I'm not going to attempt to give you specific directions in this area.

I do, however, want to stress the importance of caring and understanding when you recognize that an employee is going through a difficult time. As always, your primary goal should be to help the employee solve or eliminate the problem. Personal issues, however, are often beyond your control. And many times, employees don't want your help.

About the best advice I can give you is to be supportive of your employees without jeopardizing the security of other employees and of the company as a whole.

TIP #9: *Know your rights*

Be sure of your rights as a manager. Occasionally, you will encounter touchy situations that could end up in court. For example, you might have an employee who just isn't working out in the job. After several attempts to modify that person's behavior through constructive methods, you may decide you have to terminate or transfer the employee. Make sure you are following regulations before you do anything. As a supervisor, you're a primary link in the disciplinary system. If you handle a situation incorrectly, the company is liable. You cannot afford to make mistakes in this area.

Ask the personnel director, if your organization has one, about labor laws that apply to your position. If you don't have a personnel department, talk to your superior about the issue of labor laws.

Key Points

▶ Evaluations may seem like a major headache but, if you do them correctly, you as a supervisor can draw many benefits from conducting formal appraisals.

(1) The process of effectively evaluating employees forces you to focus on your workers as individuals.

(2) Formal appraisal interviews give supervisors and their employees an opportunity to discuss important issues in depth.

(3) By conducting effective evaluations, you communicate your commitment to developing your employees to their fullest potential.

(4) Formal evaluations provide objective records necessary for making critical personnel decisions.

▶ Effective evaluations are founded on understanding. To build a positive attitude toward evaluations, educate your employees.

(1) Make sure employees understand that you have a positive attitude toward evaluations.

(2) Educate your employees on exactly how your system works.

(3) Describe for employees the role you play in enabling them to reach peak performance. Let them know you accept some responsibility for their performance.

▶ Several pointers can make your evaluation interviews more productive.

(1) Emphasize the positive.

(2) Focus on objectives.

(3) Be honest and candid.

(4) Keep all interviews on a mature, professional level.

(5) Invite and facilitate a two-way exchange.

(6) Close evaluation interviews with a plan of action.

▶ Performance counseling is more effective than discipline or punishment for attempting to correct special problems with employees. When trying to help employees work through their problems, these tips can improve your effectiveness:

(1) Before you confront an employee with a problem, make sure you have all the facts.

(2) Make sure your employees are informed about the problem or issue.

(3) Discuss any problems with employees as soon as possible after you notice them.

(4) Be frank and open with employees about problems affecting their work.

(5) Focus on the behavior or issue, not on the employee.

(6) Be consistent.

(7) Keep your superior informed of serious discipline or behavior problems.

(8) Handle special employee problems with care.

(9) Know your rights.

Self-Development Steps

(1) If your company currently has a formal evaluation system, what can you, as a supervisor administering the system, do to maximize its effectiveness for your employees?

(2) If your company has no formal evaluation system, design one you can use for your employees. If your system works, you may want to consider proposing it to your superiors.

CHAPTER

9

AS THE HOUR GLASS TRICKLES
Filling Your Time With Meaning

"We are always preparing to live, and never living."

— Henry David Thoreau

Most management and professional development books include chapters on time management. These chapters are usually bulging with ideas on packing more activities into less time, building time-saving habits and ridding your schedule of time wasters.

Getting the most from your time, however, is more than mastering a few tactics and techniques. Time is life, or, as Benjamin Franklin said, it's "the stuff life is made of." Time is not days on a calendar, hours on a clock, or squares on a daily planner. Those standards only measure the passing of our lives. Time is the continuous flow of our existence.

To fill time with meaning is to fill life with meaning — and that's a bit more complicated than efficiently scheduling appointments and chores.

I'm not going to attempt to answer the question, "What is the meaning of life?" I'll leave that arduous task to gurus perched on mountaintops. But if time is "the stuff life is made of," I think we have to explore the concept of building meaning into our lives before we can talk about the basic how-to's of managing our time most efficiently.

Let's touch on some basics that might help you take charge of your life and help you take better control of the way you spend your time.

Invest Your Time Wisely

Most of us waste our time more recklessly than we would ever consider wasting our money.

Many people trade the present in pursuit of the future. For example, when I was in the Army, I knew many people who found little satisfaction in the 20 years they spent in the military. Yet, they stayed with it because they liked the retirement plan. They sacrificed time.

Other people wrap themselves in immediate pleasures today without giving much thought to tomorrow. They are likely to wake up one day and ask themselves, "What do I have to show for the past 20 years? What has been the point of my existence?" They fritter away their time.

I've also known people, the most unfortunate, who seem incapable of finding satisfaction in the present or the future. They are caught in jobs that make them miserable; yet they have no plans for improvement or escape. They simply plod through each day aimlessly and joylessly. They kill time.

A special few, however, capture the power and the excitement that comes from enjoying today in pursuits that will build a better tomorrow. These people use their time to the fullest.

Their lives flow in what I call *fulfillment* time.

A writer who loves the challenge of creating characters and scenes with words while writing an insightful and entertaining story is living in fulfillment time. An accountant who happily crunches numbers while building an independent accounting firm is living in fulfillment time. A supervisor who enjoys working with the employees and strives to develop a strong and growing team is living in fulfillment time.

These people fill their time and their lives with meaning, because they are pursuing a worthy destination while enjoying the journey. Both the ends and the means bring them satisfaction. Katherine Graham, publisher of the **The Washington Post,** once made a statement that captures the essence of fulfillment time. She said, "To love what you do and feel that it matters — how could anything be more fun?"[20]

Few would argue with her. So why doesn't everyone live this way? Because it may sound simple, but it's not easy to achieve. I know very few people who live in fulfillment time. Most of us fall into one of the three categories I described earlier. We sacrifice our best years — the "prime" of our lives — for a secure, yet unimpressive, future goal. Or we fritter away the present on aimless pursuits of pleasure. Or we let feelings of powerlessness and despair consume our lives.

The reasons people fail to fill their lives with meaning through fulfillment time are countless and complex. Our backgrounds, our fears and insecurities, and our misconceptions all have an impact on the way we live our lives. I believe in the power of education, however. Once people understand that they can change their lives, they can enjoy themselves in the present while pursuing their goals. They can begin to get the most from their time.

You, too, can learn how to fill your time with meaning!

How To Build Fulfillment Time Into Your Life

As a supervisor, how can you build fulfillment time in your life? By seeking fulfillment in your career.

What is it about being a supervisor that appeals to you? Is it the opportunity to work with people; to mold a raw young talent into a proficient and productive asset to the company? The chance to develop a process; to bring order out of chaos and thus contribute to the company's profitability?

Here are some strategies you can follow in developing ways to find fulfillment time in your job as supervisor:

STRATEGY #1: *Define the purpose of your work*

Many supervisors think the purpose of their work is spelled out for them — to get their employees to get the work done. They figure they have no control over their purpose. I disagree.

Certainly, on the surface, it would appear that your purpose is limited by your job description. You may have a long list of duties and responsibilities, and your superiors may hand you a ready-made purpose, such as, "To coordinate and oversee the smooth and productive operation of first-shift employees in the shipping room."

Those formal guidelines, however, usually don't address the broad role you fill for the company. When you get past the words, you serve a vital purpose. You are the force behind the wheels of action. Upper management sets the direction for the organization, and you fuel the company's progress by organizing and motivating your team for maximum productivity. Your purpose is not the sum total of your tasks and duties. Your purpose is to maintain the business' strength in the marketplace by enabling your team to produce at full capacity. The role you play is vital to your company's security and success.

Isn't the knowledge of your significance energizing? Knowing that your work matters is vital to feeling fulfilled. So look beyond your job description to find the purpose in your work. Consider the impact you have on your company's performance in the marketplace. You are a key to their success.

In addition to the purpose you serve for the company, you also have a personal purpose — personal career goals. You are a supervisor today, but where do you want to be five years from now? As you contribute to your company's prosperity, have a clear picture of the progress you would like to make as a professional. Set a goal that fulfills your needs as an individual. Of course, your personal goals need to match your purpose as supervisor. As you work to meet one, you move closer to filling the other.

Focusing on your purpose — both for the company and for yourself — gives your work meaning. You can see how the steps you take today will have an impact on the quality of your life tomorrow. You are filled with a sense of mission.

STRATEGY #2: *Design a plan for filling that purpose*

Once you have your purpose clearly in focus, design a strategy for fulfilling that purpose. If your purpose is to get maximum output from your employees, ask yourself, "What's it going to take to enable my people to achieve peak performance?"

Let's say you've reviewed the troops and you decide that to get maximum productivity you have to increase your employees' skills, improve team morale and get more cooperation from other departments. Those are your goals. What do you have to do accomplish each of those objectives? Your response to this question will suggest a plan for addressing each issue.

For example, to increase employee skills, your plan might be to design an effective training system. Set a goal for creating and implementing a training program for your employees.

To improve morale, your plan might be to improve your relationship with employees.

To build cooperation among the different departments, your plan could be to set up regular meetings with representatives from each department to discuss and design ways the departments could work together more effectively.

Let me share with you a few tips for setting goals and designing plans so that you actually reach your objectives.

First of all, make your goals measurable. "Develop employee skills" is vague. To put punch into your goals, be specific. "Increase each employee's productivity by at least 25% through skill development" is much more effective.

Second, break your goals down into sub-goals. I have what I call long-range goals, intermediate goals and short-range goals. A goal for improving employee skills is long-range. "Design customized training system for 100 employees to improve their equipment operation skills" is an example of an intermediate goal. "Hold training session at 10 a.m. Friday" could be the short-range goal.

Intermediate and short-range goals allow you to break your goals down into manageable steps. That way, you are more likely to follow through on them. Staring a long-range goal in the face can be overwhelming. You don't know where to start or what to do. Short-range goals give you a handle on your objectives.

Third, write your goals down, and set a deadline for each one. For example, you can write:

Begin training May 1.

Know each employee personally by Aug. 15.

<u>Establish regular inter-departmental meetings by July 1.</u>

Writing your goals and assigning each one a deadline gives them weight. You will feel more committed to follow through on them. When your goals are in black and white, you can look at them often, and they will motivate you to keep working and striving to attain them. Writing your goals down also improves your planning. You can look at your long-range goals each week and plan your activities according to what you want to accomplish.

Meeting a purpose means having a plan of action. So always design strategies for fulfilling your purpose.

Let me share a bit of advice with you here: For your goals to have impact, they must be challenging, yet attainable. You want your goals to force you to stretch and grow. But if you consistently set goals that you cannot achieve no matter how hard you work, you will only create frustration, which can have a destructive effect on your employees' development and growth. Pursue challenges realistically.

For example, let's say your goal is to improve your employees' skills. To expect your team to double its production in one week because of increased skills is unrealistic. You'd be setting up the group for failure. You would damage morale and production.

A more realistic and inspiring goal might be to increase team output by 25% over a six-month period. This goal gives people a concrete and attainable target toward which to aim.

When you focus on ways to fulfill your purpose, don't overlook the objective in your personal life. It's important to set goals for all areas of your life. Develop goals for your career, your home and family life, your social life, your community and your personal development, and you will find satisfaction in life — not just on the job. When you think of your community, think of it in the expansive sense. It's the neighborhood in which you live, but it's also your city, your state, the nation, other nations, the world. With the modern-day shrinkage of time and space, the entire Earth is your community. Begin with your own back yard, but look for ways that you can make your contribution to the entire community of mankind.

STRATEGY #3: *Implement your goals*

Take action! Once you know what needs to be done and how you are going to do it, get to work.

Attack each task or chore you have set for yourself with enthusiasm. Remember, as you complete each one, you are another step closer to your goals.

One pointer for getting to more of your goals each day: **Start with the undesirable tasks first.** That way, when you finish those chores, you will still feel energized to jump into what you really like to do.

For example, maybe you have a dreaded monthly report that needs to be completed tomorrow. But you also have several ideas you want to propose to your team and get some feedback on. You're anticipating an interesting discussion. Take care of the report first. Get it off your back and out of your mind. Then move on to the job you really like — working more closely with your employees.

Another pointer: **Spend your most productive time on your most challenging tasks.** If you're at your best before lunch, set that time aside for the projects that require concentration.

Keeping a goal journal will also help you follow through on your goals. Regularly record your progress toward a goal. Write about the forward strides, and write about the obstacles you hit. Writing about your progress can inspire you to keep working. Writing about the obstacles in your way can help you define problems and move you closer to finding solutions.

In addition to writing about your progress, **visualize the realization of your goals.** See your employees working smoothly at highly-skilled jobs. Picture your team sharing a strong spirit. Imagine your department working closely with other departments to reach company objectives. Have detailed images in your mind of your goals in action.

These visualizations will keep the goal alive in your mind and will help you maintain a strong commitment to following through on your strategies.

STRATEGY #4: *Review your progress on a regular basis*

As you work, stand back occasionally and look at your achievements. This process serves several purposes.

For one thing, it builds in you a sense of accomplishment. You can see the results of your labor. Reviewing your successes, then, motivates you to continue working hard and moving toward your goals.

Secondly, you can examine your results and efforts and look for ways to improve. You learn from your mistakes only when you take the time to recognize them. You can also judge whether you're drifting off the course you've set for reaching your goals. If so, you can make the necessary adjustments.

Third, stepping away from your work will give you a chance to relax a little. Then you can approach your mission later with a fresh, rejuvenated attitude.

Take Control Of Your Time By Taking Control Of Yourself

When your work has meaning and you feel a sense of purpose, you will automatically begin to do more in less time. You will feel a drive to accomplish everything necessary to reach your goals and achieve your purpose.

I want to share with you now two suggestions that can give you more time to pursue the goals that are important to you.

SUGGESTION #1: *Get organized*

Disorganization probably eats up more productive time than any other single factor. When we're disorganized, we spend countless hours deciding what we need to do next, how to do it, where to get the tools to do it and so on. Getting organized is not really that difficult. As a matter of fact, once you get your work in order, you'll find staying organized much easier than trying to function in disorganized surroundings.

Here are a few rules that can help you get — and stay — organized:

(1) Cultivate decisiveness. Don't let unmade decisions clutter your mind and make it difficult to concentrate on other problems. Handle decisions as they develop.

When an issue comes up, determine what information or input you need to make a decision. For example, do you need more information? If so, get it. Do you need to involve others in the decision? Contact them as soon as possible. Do you have to wait for other conditions to develop before you can make the decision? For example, would it be wise for you wait and see how a related issue is handled in another department?

Once you have all the facts and information, weigh the pros and cons of the various options. Think through the results of your decision. What kind of reactions can you expect?

After analyzing your alternatives, make your decision. Then track the results. Ask yourself these questions:

❱ Did things work out as I expected them to?

❱ Did any problems arise from my decision?

❱ How could those problems have been avoided?

❱ Can I learn anything from this experience that will help me make more effective decisions in the future?

When making decisions, don't get hung up on trying to be perfect. You will inevitably make mistakes. Everyone does. But you will never get things right if you refuse to make decisions. So be willing to take risks. Get the facts and decide.

Once you've made a decision, let it go. Sure, you can learn from it, but don't dwell on it, rehashing it in your mind. Learn and move on.

(2) Arrange your paperwork for efficiency. Keep your desk cleared of papers by handling each piece only once. Throw away, file, pass on to someone else, take action, or whatever, but deal with the message or memo the first time you pick it up. Answer letters, notes or memos by writing responses at the bottom of the page. Sometimes it's appropriate to return that copy to the sender. Otherwise, type a neat response as soon as you can after receiving the correspondence.

Keep your letters short. One paragraph is fine. Plan what you want to say and say it as succinctly as possible.

(3) Keep your environment in order. Know where everything is on your desk. Keep your files organized. Replace files as soon as you are finished using them. Stress the importance of an organized work environment to your employees. Ask that they keep the work area free of clutter, and that they keep supplies, files or any other materials or equipment they access in neat condition.

(4) Master your feelings. Emotions are a part of being human. Sometimes you might not feel like doing your best or getting your work done. On those days when you'd rather be sailing, resist the urge. Instead, focus on what you have to do. Focus on reaching your purpose. Recalling the feelings of accomplishment you experienced when you completed other jobs that held little excitement can also help you get back on track. Whatever you do, don't give in to feelings of despair. Remember the laws of inertia: An object in motion tends to stay in motion; an object at rest tends to stay at rest.

SUGGESTION #2: *Develop time-saving habits*

Someone once said, "There's no way on earth to save time. All you can do is spend it." Spend your time wisely by developing some of these habits:

Habit #1: Concentrate on results, not on activities. Think of your work in terms of what you want to accomplish, not just what you are going to do. For example, maybe you have to organize your employees' evaluation reports for year-end appraisal interviews. Don't say to yourself, "I'll work on these reports for one hour." Instead say, "I'll finish 10 reports before going to lunch." That way, you focus on getting work done, rather than watching the clock.

Habit #2: Put yourself on a carefully planned work schedule. Write a list of everything you want to do, and rank the items in order of priority. Estimating as realistically as possible how long each task will take, set deadlines for achieving each objective. Then, go down the list one by one. As soon as you are finished with one item, move on to the next. If you get hung up on one item, leave it temporarily and move to something that can be done in the meantime.

Habit #3: Do things right the first time. Don't waste time going back and correcting your work. Making the effort to do things right in the beginning will save you time in the long run.

Habit #4: Don't get blown away in the information explosion. Share reading with others. Talk to your peers and superiors about books and articles they have read and pick their minds for the important details. When sharing a book or magazine, highlight important areas. When reading a book, read only the chapters or sections that are pertinent to you.

Eliminate information distractions. Cancel publication subscriptions that don't provide helpful information. Get off mailing lists.

Rather than reading, listen to tapes in your car or while you're doing other things.

Habit #5: Do everything on schedule or as soon as you can. In other words, don't procrastinate. Don't look for excuses to avoid unpleasant work; just get to it. I found a great description of procrastination: "The invitation to procrastinate often comes dressed as an urgent chore."[21] I'm guilty of using "more important tasks" as an excuse for not doing something that I just didn't want to do. That little trick can eat up a lot of your time. Don't put off chores; just do them.

Habit #6: Use your telephone time efficiently. Before you start dialing numbers, make a list of what you want to say. When the other person answers, get to the point. Don't get caught in a lot of social chit-chat.

You can also save a great deal of time by screening your calls. If you don't have a secretary, sometimes you can use an answering machine. If possible, schedule a specific time during the day when you will accept calls. It's just as wise to schedule telephone appointments as it is to schedule visits from people.

Habit #7: Work every minute on scheduled results. Make sure everything you do has a purpose and contributes to your mission to meet your objectives.

Habit #8: Take breaks only when you need them. Don't feel like you have to take a scheduled break just because the whistle blows. Keep working when you've built up your momentum. Take breaks when you are between tasks or when you need to take a breather.

Habit #9: Learn to say "no." Don't take on more than you can handle. If you do, you will end up wasting time because you won't be able to give any of your projects the attention each deserves.

Habit #10: Keep interruptions and distractions to a minimum. Make time for concentrating on your work, and schedule a specific time when people can interrupt you. It's also a good idea to go to see people in their work areas. That way, you don't have to wait for them to leave your office. If someone drops in while you're trying to get some work done, stand up to talk to them. That's a polite signal that you don't have a lot of time for chit-chat.

Habit #11: Systematize all routine activities. For example, use standard letters when possible and follow a set formula for reports.

Key Points

▶ Filling your time with meaning depends on filling your life with meaning.

▶ To fill your time and life with meaning requires that you pursue a worthy destination along an enjoyable route. Both the journey and the goal bring you satisfaction.

▶ Here is a strategy for building more fulfillment into your work and your life:

(1) Define the purpose of your work.

(2) Design a plan for filling that purpose.

(3) Implement your goals.

(4) Review your progress on a regular basis.

▶ Take control of your time by taking control of yourself.

(1) Get organized.

(2) Develop time-saving habits.

Self-Development Steps

(1) If you don't have a sense of purpose in your work, you need to find one before you can begin to live in fulfillment time. Examine yourself, your position and your life and begin the task of determining your purpose. This might not happen in a day, a month or even a year. But, it's vital that you arrive at a purpose.

(2) List any time-wasting habits you have, and develop a plan for replacing them with time-saving habits.

CHAPTER

10

KEEPING
HUMPTY DUMPTY
TOGETHER
Managing the Stress of
Supervisory Leadership

"Complete freedom from stress is death."

— Dr. Hans Selye

Putting Humpty Dumpty together again is no guarantee that he will stay together. The newly assembled shell is going to be subjected to the rigors of global competition. That means stress on your organization. That means stress on you.

The supervisor's job description should include the phrase, **"Manage stress effectively,"** right along with **"Evaluate employee**

performance" and **"Distribute assignments."** As a supervisor, you hold one of the most stressful positions in corporate America. The pressures of your work can be tremendous if you are committed to achieving excellence and to enabling your team to maintain peak performance.

Consider just a few of the obvious major stressors supervisors in all industries face:
▶ Meeting your company's high standards of excellence.
▶ Balancing responsibilities to superiors with responsibilities to subordinates.
▶ Maintaining a high level of production in your department.
▶ Investing a part of yourself in relationships with each of your employees.
▶ Coping with the frustrations that inevitably accompany a supervisor's limited authority.[22]
▶ Striving to reach personal career goals.
▶ Doing tedious but necessary jobs, such as paper work.
▶ Balancing the demands of your professional life with those of your personal life.

Management at any level, of course, is stressful. Leaders — from shop supervisors to CEOs — shoulder tremendous responsibility for the well-being of the company and the security of the people who make up the organization. This pressure is constant and many times intense.

Supervisors who aspire to produce positive results for their companies, their employees and themselves must learn to recognize the stress in their lives — not just on their jobs — and to manage it in a way that enhances rather than weakens their performances.

Understanding The Dynamics Of Stress

Dr. Hans Selye, an authority on tension, defined stress as the "non-specific response of the body to any demand placed on it, whether that demand is shocking grief or pleasant relief." In other words, stress is not what happens to us; it's our response to what happens to us. External forces don't generate the stress in our lives; it's our perceptions of and reactions to the outside influences that burn us out.

For example, how would you react if your superior walked into your office and said, "Your department has to double its output this week. XYZ Inc. needs a double shipment"? Would you become angry? Would you focus on the impossibility of meeting such an unreasonable deadline? Would you argue with your boss, or sit and stew in your resentment?

Or would you accept the assignment as a challenge? Would you be glad orders were up? Would you immediately start focusing on ways to reach the demanding goal? Would you see the increased business as an opportunity to test yourself and your team and to prove to upper management that you can produce?

The way you react to the events around you determines the level of stress in your life. You can rarely control what happens around you and to you. You have no direct control over the volume of work the sales department creates. But you can control how you react.

Certainly, the quality of the work you and your team produce has an impact on your company's ability to maintain strong customer relationships. You can't, however, control sales. You have no way to determine when your team will be asked to double production, or to cut back output (which probably creates even more stress).

185

The only element you can control is yourself. You can control your response. If a piece of equipment breaks down, you can choose to get angry, to yell at your employees and to have a general fit. Or you can start looking for a solution. If your superior passes along a seemingly impossible assignment to your crew, you can stew silently, or you can discuss alternatives with your boss.

You control the level of stress you experience by controlling your reactions to the events happening to you and around you. Face it. You cannot eliminate the events that cause stress. You can't control economic trends that can put a stranglehold on your company and jeopardize your job. You can't prevent personal tragedies. Things happen. That's life.

You can, however, control your responses to those events. You can be the master of your fate by taking responsibility for your reaction to situations and circumstances. When you accept this responsibility, you can reduce the negative effects of stress in your life. And those effects can be devastating.

Stress is usually the culprit behind such physical afflictions as headaches, neck and back aches, nervous stomachs and ulcers, insomnia, heart disease and hypertension, and weakened immunity to infections. Stress can also manifest itself in bouts of irritability and depression, low sexual desire, and eating disorders, such as loss of appetite or overeating.

Those complications, however, are only the negative effects of stress.

Pressure also has a positive side. Stress, to a certain degree, is a necessary ingredient for a fulfilling life. Exciting opportunities are wrapped up within the pressures you face as a supervisor:

opportunities for personal growth and achievement, opportunities to help others realize their potential, and opportunities to make a significant contribution to your company. Dr. Donald Tubesing, author of **Kicking Your Stress Habits,** compares the stress in our lives to the tension in a violin string: "It needs enough tension to make music, but not to snap."

Can you imagine going through a day without any challenges? Picture waking up in the morning with no pressures to be any-where or to accomplish anything. Let's say you're financially independent. You don't **have** to do anything. How long do you think you could last under those circumstances? It might sound nice for a few days. But humans aren't programmed for stagna-tion.

Even most people who are born into extravagant wealth do not wallow in their affluence, wasting their lives on hollow pursuits (although you can find tragic biographies on the few who have). No matter what our stations in life, most of us are driven, as if by instinct, to do something meaningful — to pursue a career, support a social cause, have a family, or whatever. We feel compelled to be a part of something bigger than simply existing day to day.

Pursuing a goal or filling a purpose, as we talked about in Chapter Nine, is a positive pressure — the kind of stress that brings out our best. I've heard people say again and again that they work better under pressure. Most of us do. All of us need some pressure, some tension, to give our lives meaning.

As a supervisor, you can't eliminate the stress in your life, and, even if you could, completely erasing personal tension can be as harmful as living under too much stress. The key to functioning at top capacity is to learn to manage stress; to use it as a positive force.

How To Manage Effectively The Stress In Your Life— On And Off The Job

Sometimes our stresses don't cause as many problems as do our "solutions." Some people attempt to escape stress through alcohol and drugs, including even prescription and over-the-counter medications, such as tranquilizers or sleeping pills. This line of defense, however, usually leads to despair.

Some people withdraw mentally. They go through the motions of a job or a relationship, but they are not really involved. They don't invest any part of themselves in their work. They are there in body only, not in spirit. Some acute cases of withdrawal develop into mental illness.

Neither escape nor withdrawal offers a very attractive solution. Either can lead to more serious problems than the events or circumstances creating the stress in the first place.

Coping with stress in a healthful manner involves a two-pronged strategy.

In addition to learning to control your responses to the events and situations that are beyond your control, you can take charge of your life and eliminate the stressors over which you do have some control. For example, taking care of yourself both physically and emotionally can give you the energy and strength to handle stressful conditions that you have no power over. Being in control of yourself gives you tremendous power.

There's a story about two sisters who grew up in a household headed by an alcoholic father. One of the women never drank and became a tremendous success. The other turned to alcohol for solace and stumbled from crisis to crisis. The women explained their reaction to growing up under stress with the same reasoning, "When you look at my father, is it any wonder I turned out this way?"

One sister took control of her life; the other let circumstances control her.

If you want to reduce the stress in your life, take control of yourself. I have discovered over the years several techniques for maintaining control in life and building strong coping mechanisms:

TECHNIQUE #1: *Develop realistic expectations*

As a supervisor committed to excellence, you may be demanding too much of yourself and of the people around you.

High achievers have a real problem with this technique. They like to think of themselves as supermen and superwomen. That's a design for disaster.

When you expect too much of yourself, you usually overcommit. You believe you can accomplish more than is possible for any human. You are constantly struggling to meet deadlines and obligations. This pattern can stress out the most energetic supervisor. That's when the quality of your work falls off. And when you're dissatisfied with your work, you feel like a failure.

The tendency to expect too much from yourself almost always carries over into your expectations of other people. You think to yourself, "If I can work 75 hours a week for a month, so can my employees (superiors, colleagues, etc)." When people fail to meet your expectations, you become frustrated. Your anger will then begin to erode your relationships. Everyone will suffer under the tension you create through unrealistic expectations.

Know yourself and know the people you work with. Set reasonable, realistic goals. Certainly, you want to challenge yourself and your team to stretch and grow, but don't make unrealistic demands. When people repeatedly fail to meet expectations, their stress levels rise and their morale suffers.

TECHNIQUE #2: *Stay in touch with yourself*

Try to define the events or circumstances in your life that cause you stress, and reduce or eliminate them wherever possible. Find out what bugs you and learn to deal with it.

For example, if you know that getting a slow start in the mornings makes you feel hurried and tense the rest of the day, get to work a few minutes early. That way, you can avoid the coffee-pot conversation that delays the start of your work day.

Or let's say your employees are quitting 10 minutes before the end of the day and standing around. That behavior is driving you crazy. Talk to them about it. Don't let the action continue while you stew. Do something.

Seek to identify and understand what causes you stress, and find ways to reduce or eliminate it.

TECHNIQUE #3: *Take time to meditate*

An insurance company in Holland reduced its premiums 30% for people who meditate. A study the company conducted demonstrated some amazing facts relating to people who practiced meditation.

They found that meditation reduces the risk of:
- Heart disease by 87%.
- Infectious diseases by 30%.
- Benign and malignant tumors by 55%.
- Diseases of the nervous system by 87%.

How to meditate is a personal decision for each individual. I've been meditating since 1973, and it's made a tremendous difference in my life.

Find a method you are comfortable with.

TECHNIQUE #4: *Cultivate self-discipline and self-control*

We create a lot of our own stress. Our habits and lifestyles sometimes set us up for pressure situations. For example, we may take out a loan to buy a recreational vehicle, and then feel strained to meet the payment. Or we might spend too much time doing non-essential things, then feel under pressure to complete the vital tasks.

We can reduce a great deal of our stress by examining our values and cultivating self-discipline. Here are three ways to reduce stress:

▶ Do what needs to be done when you need to do it. Procrastination is a major stress-builder that we inflict on ourselves. Don't wait until you have only three days to complete a project assigned one month in advance.

▶ Be willing to say "no." Some of the most stressed out people I know are the ones who can never turn down a request. For example, a supervisor asks a colleague if she will file his weekly reports for him on Friday because he's leaving early for vacation. She agrees. Then an employee asks for assistance on a project, and dumps the entire mess in her lap. She accepts the burden without complaint. A friend in another department calls and asks her to do some research on a project, and she says, "yes." By the end of the week, she's worn to a frazzle trying to meet her own obligations and do these favors for others.

As a supervisor, you probably have enough work in meeting your own responsibilities. Be cooperative, but take a stand. Be willing to say "no" when people make unreasonable demands. This goes for your personal life as well.

▶ Do things right the first time. It's tempting to rush through a job, especially if you are already under time pressure. But the results are usually counterproductive. Many times, hurried work is unacceptable and has to be redone. I agree with Howard W. Newton, who said, "People forget how fast you did a job — but they remember how well you did it."[23]

Take the time to do things right the first time, and you will experience less stress for at least two reasons: You will feel better about yourself, and you will save time.

TECHNIQUE #5: *Follow your own judgment*

You are in the position of supervisor because you know how to do the job and because your superiors have confidence in you. So make your own decisions. Do what you feel is right in each situation you face. Don't let others pressure you. Stick to your values and convictions.

You reduce stress when you take responsibility for your actions and your attitudes by following your own judgment. You will always have the secure feeling of knowing that you have done what you thought was best.

I'm not suggesting you should never ask your superiors or people with more experience or expertise than you for advice. It's important, however, that you understand that you are ultimately responsible for what you do and say. So after considering advice from others and all the information at your disposal, follow your own judgment.

TECHNIQUE #6: *Cultivate a sense of humor*

Laughter really **is** the best medicine. Sometimes all you can do is laugh when things aren't going as smoothly as you like. A sense of humor will help you maintain your sanity when machines malfunction, employees clash, your workload doubles and the coffee maker spits muddy water.

Learn to laugh at absurd situations. Be able to laugh at yourself. And be willing to laugh with others. Laughter refreshes and lightens the burdens of responsibilities. Exercise your funny bone regularly.

TECHNIQUE #7: *Maintain a positive mental attitude*

Volumes have been written on the power of a positive mental attitude. It works.

When you start feeding positive thoughts and influences into your mind, you will begin to see opportunities where once you saw hopelessness. You will find potential in people you had dismissed as helpless. And, you will find a reserve of strength and energy within yourself that you never would have imagined was there.

Like a good sense of humor, positive thinking helps you focus on what you can accomplish, rather than on your problems.

When you have a positive mental attitude, you feel better about yourself, your work and the people around you. You feel energized.

TECHNIQUE #8: *Match tasks to energy levels*

Get to know yourself, and match your work to your energy level. This habit alone will reduce a great deal of stress. Once you understand when you are at peak energy levels, you will know when to schedule your most challenging tasks. When you are barely chugging along, take care of simpler chores.

For example, I know that right after lunch, at about 2 p.m., I'm tired. I just don't have the zest I feel in the morning. So, that's when I do things like read my mail or return phone calls or some activity that requires physical involvement. I don't try to start on a project that demands mental creativity.

TECHNIQUE #9: *Don't be a perfectionist*

Perfection is not possible. Aiming for perfection in anything is a prescription for frustration and stress. Instead, aim for excellence.

Shoot for doing the best job you can do. It may not be perfect, but you will have the satisfaction of knowing you tried your best. And do you want to know something? When you are committed to excellence — and I mean you really strive to do your best — you usually come pretty close to perfection.

TECHNIQUE #10: *Accept when you have no control*

Let's say your boss announces to you, "We have to lay off 500 people companywide. Ten of those cuts are going to be in your department. By the end of the week, we need from you a recommendation on whom to release." That's a stressful situation. But it's beyond your control.

If you've been meeting your responsibilities as a supervisor and you and your team have made an all-out contribution to the company's production, you've done all you can do. Agonizing over the fact that 10 of your workers are going to be out of jobs will serve no purpose. Accept the reality of the situation, and move on.

The best you can do is make the situation as easy as possible for everyone involved. Focus on making fair assessments of your employees and choosing the right people for the layoffs. Determine what you can do to make the transition as painless as possible, both for the people the company is letting go and for those employees who must produce in the environment of uncertainty and fear that layoffs always create.

Recognize situations and events that are beyond your control, and focus on the elements you can control.

TECHNIQUE #11: *Maintain good physical condition*

Your physical condition has a tremendous impact on your mental and emotional states and on your ability to cope with stress.

To be able to handle the stress of being a supervisor, it's important you eat right, get proper rest and exercise regularly.

The condition of your body will affect the ability of your mind and emotions to process through and manage the stresses in your life.

In addition to making you better able to cope with tension, exercise can actually reduce the stress you feel.[24] The scientific explanation, in case you're interested, is: A good workout releases endorphins in your brain. These hormones then trigger a relaxation response. Have you ever heard of a runner's high? That heady feeling is caused by endorphins.

If you exercise regularly and are in good physical condition, your brain will automatically release endorphins when you feel stress. That becomes your body's response to any demand placed on it, whether the demand is completing a road race or meeting a deadline.

Get in shape, and not only will you feel better physically, but you'll also be stronger mentally and emotionally.

TECHNIQUE #12: *Celebrate your successes*

You can reduce the stress you feel by rejuvenating your spirit with a celebration once in a while. If you are doing things right and meeting the goals you've set for yourself and your team, you deserve to kick back and enjoy the positive feelings success produces.

Celebrations and rewards help you maintain a balanced perspective. Your work is not all stress and drudgery. It is also accomplishment and satisfaction. And celebrations should be shared. Some of the activities mentioned in Chapter Six can be turned into celebrations or recognition dinners. "Hey, guys, we ought to buy Carol's burger tonight since she beat all production records last week when we had that double order," gives a different tone to the weekly bowling night.

TECHNIQUE #13: *Learn to relax*

For some, relaxation can take place looking at a sunset, sitting on the top of a mountain, listening to soft, soothing music, or being in a hot tub.

But sometimes we don't have the relaxation techniques right at hand.

One way you can relax is to go into a quiet room, sit in a comfortable chair, keep your feet on the floor, undo tight buttons, close your eyes and take a few deep breaths until you're aware that you're beginning to relax. You can tighten your muscles from the top of your head to the bottom of your feet. This is best done in sessions: Tighten your facial muscles all together, then relax, and repeat; next, tighten your shoulder muscles, relax and repeat. Continue through the rest of your body. Once you have relaxed your body, travel in your mind's eye to your favorite place, where it is very peaceful. Stay there for 10 to 20 minutes. If you have a problem that needs to be solved, bring it here and see if any solutions come to mind. If none appear, don't worry. Let them go, and just relax and be with your favorite quiet place.

When your time is completed, start being aware of the room around you — the noise, the smells, etc., and when you are ready, open your eyes.

Do note that it is better not to do this right after a heavy meal. The effect won't be as significant.

Studies show that the relaxation exercise is effective for relieving inner tension, lowering blood pressure and improving physical and mental health.

Key Points

▶ Stress is not what happens to us; it's our reactions to the events in our lives. When we learn to control our reactions, we can control the level of stress we experience.
▶ A certain amount of stress is a necessary ingredient for a fulfilling life. Exciting challenges and opportunities are wrapped up within the pressures you face as a supervisor.
▶ If you want to reduce the destructive stress in your life, take control.

(1) Develop realistic expectations of yourself, of others and of life in general.

(2) Stay in touch with yourself.

(3) Take time to meditate.

(4) Cultivate self-discipline and self-control.

(5) Follow your own judgment.

(6) Cultivate a sense of humor.

(7) Maintain a positive mental attitude.

(8) Match tasks to energy levels.

(9) Don't be a perfectionist.

(10) Recognize and accept when you have no control over a situation.

(11) Maintain good physical condition.

(12) Celebrate your successes.

(13) Learn to relax.

Self-Development Section

(1) Identify and list the main stressors in your life. Put a check by any stressors that are self-inflicted. For example, you may have too many demands placed on you because you don't know when to say "no."

(2) Using the list from exercise #1, develop a strategy for eliminating the unnecessary stressors in your life.

1 Warren Bennis, *On Becoming a Leader*
(Reading, MA: Addison-Wesley Publishing Co., Inc., 1989), p. 4.

2 Warren Bennis and Burt Nanus, Leaders, *The Strategies for Taking Charge*
(New York: Harper and Row, Publishers, 1985), p. 44.

3 Peter Block, *The Empowered Manager*
(San Francisco, CA: Jossey-Bass Inc., 1987), p. xiii.

4 Block, p. 23.

5 We'll discuss this in greater detail in the chapter on delegation.

6 Motivational Quotes
(Lombard, IL: Great Quotations, Inc.), p. M5.

7 Motivational Quotes, p. M38.

8 New World Dictionary, Second College Edition
(New York: Simon and Schuster, 1980), p. 287.

9 I've changed the names to protect the innocent.

10 Roger M. D'Aprix, *The Believable Corporation* (New York: AMACOM, a division of American Management Associations, 1977), pp. 43-45.

11 Donna Vinton, "Delegation for Employee Development," *Training and Development Journal,* January 1987, p. 65.

12 Marion Hayes, *Stepping Up to Supervisor*
(Houston, TX: Executive Roundtable Publications, 1987), p. 148.

13 Robert B. Maddux, *Team Building, An Exercise in Leadership,*
(Los Altos, California: Crisp Publications, Inc., 1986,) p.5

14 Wolf J. Rinke, Ph.D., "Empowering Your Team Members," *Supervisory Management* (April 1989), p. 21.

15 Motivational Quotes (Lombard, IL: Great Quotations, Inc.), p. M68.

16 The Japanese invest 300% more money in each of their employees than does the United States. Moreover, supervisors generally are in charge of fewer employees.

17 Human Resource Management, volume on Personnel Practices Communications (Chicago: Commerce Clearing House Inc., 1981) pp. 3451-3458.

18 Claude S. George, Jr., *Supervision in Action: The Art of Managing Others* (Reston, VA: Reston Publishing Company, Inc., a division of Prentice-Hall, 1979), p. 134.

19 Motivational Quotes (Lombard, IL: Great Quotations, Inc.), p. M49.

20 Barbara J. Winters, as printed in Daily Development, January 1986, Vol. 1, No. 3, p. 6.

21 All supervisors occasionally hit stone walls when they present an idea or suggestion to management. This experience can be extremely frustrating when they are confident that their idea could benefit the company.

22 Motivational Quotes (Lombard, IL: Great Quotations, Inc.), p. M12.

23 Leanne Kleinmann, "The Exercise-Relaxation Connection," *Working Woman,* (April 1988), 129.

To order more books,
please check your local bookstore,
or call **1-800-345-0096.**

If you would like to receive
information about workshops
Margot Robinson conducts, please send your
name, address, and phone number to:

Margot Robinson & Associates
P.O. Box 21585
Greensboro, NC 27420

Index

A

Abilities 38, 46-47, 50-52, 60, 86, 90-91, 99, 102, 118
Accomplishments 63, 88, 117, 119, 146
Action plans 154
Alcoholism 161
Alexander the Great 24
Ambitions 63, 107, 118, 123, 138
Appraisal 143-144, 148, 149, 151, 152, 154, 162, 178
Arthur Symons 141
Assignments 6, 16, 18, 20-21, 22, 28-29, 49, 69, 84-85, 89-90
Attitudes 18-19, 27, 28, 33, 42, 46, 48, 49, 63, 66, 69, 78, 80, 93, 97
Authority 19, 27, 42-43, 85, 93, 94, 109,

B

Basic job skills 47
Behavior 20, 33, 47, 77, 112, 155-161, 164, 190
Benjamin Franklin 166
Blame 45, 83, 97, 150, 152
Body language 78-80
Boldness 39
Burt Nanus 31,
Business arena 1, 5, 18, 43, 106
Business leaders 5, 9, 14, 30, 36, 125, 136

C

Capacity 25, 49, 60, 76, 125, 142, 152, 169, 187
Capitalism 124

Career goals 151, 169, 184
Chain of command 85
Challenge 5-6, 18, 19, 33, 38, 48, 85, 87, 90-91, 106, 114, 119, 121-122, 129-130, 145, 167, 172, 185, 187, 190, 198
Challenging assignments 47
Change 4, 6, 8-11, 18, 21, 33, 42, 45, 155, 159, 168
Changing technology 4
Col. Attila 25
Col. Deadfish   25
Comfort zones   87
Commitment 6, 12, 14, 32, 38, 39, 44, 79, 113, 126-128, 131, 136, 138-139, 144-145, 151, 162, 174
Communication 55-60, 62, 66, 68, 80, 110, 132,
Concentrate 66, 75, 87, 159, 175, 178
Conceptual skills 21
Control 3, 5, 7, 10, 11, 12, 27, 29-30, 33, 41, 43, 45, 50-51 53, 55, 95, 132, 161, 166, 169, 175, 181, 185-186, 188-189, 195-196, 198-199
Convictions 33, 193
Cooperation 43, 58, 59, 90, 111, 170-171
Courage 33, 42
Creative 23, 29, 47, 115
Credit 1, 44, 72, 98, 135
Criticism 141, 147, 151-152
Cross-train 47, 129

D

David Campbell 12
Deadlines 93, 178, 189
Delegate 25, 51-52, 84-86, 88-90, 95, 96
Delegation 83, 85-88, 90-92, 94-98, 101-103
Delegator 85, 92, 95, 103
Democracy 29
Dependence 26
Develop your people 46-49, 53
Dictators 26-28, 38;
    Indentifying 27
Differing perceptions 62-63, 79
Directives 20, 56, 64, 69-70, 72
Distractions 66-68, 75, 80, 179-180
Downsizing 4, 11, 24, 42
Downward communication 72, 132
Drug abuse 161
Dynamics of leadership 24

E

Effective communication 56, 58, 69, 75
Effective leaders 35, 126-127, 138
Eggshells 2, 6, 26, 121-122
Egos 2, 6, 26, 42
Egotistical 51
Emotions and attitudes 66-67, 80
Empathy 12
Employee problems 155, 160-161, 164

Empower 9, 13, 29, 43, 44-45, 49, 53
    Empowered 41-46, 48, 53, 73
    Empowering 43, 46, 49, 53, 83,
Enable 3, 29-30, 39, 42, 47, 49, 66, 76, 85, 94, 101, 114, 126, 151, 170
Encourage 10, 28-29, 43, 47, 49, 52, 63, 72, 78, 95, 111, 114, 116, 130, 131, 154
Energized 44, 173, 194
Enthusiasm 1, 32, 48, 129, 173
Evaluations 141-149, 151, 154-155, 162
Expectations 19, 63-64, 79, 189-190, 198
External barriers 18, 62, 79-80

F

Facilitators 26, 29-30 38
Family crises 161
Fate 45, 53, 186
Feedback 26, 65, 80, 96, 173;
    Asking for 113;
    Giving and receiving 76-77;
    Soliciting 133;
Flexibility 10, 42
Follow up 96-97, 102
Formal communication 70-71
Forms of communication 70-71, 80
Freedom 5, 8, 10, 18, 26-27, 29, 43, 49, 50, 56, 63, 79, 95, 130, 183
Front line 64, 72
Fulfillment time   167-168, 181

G

Global competition 4, 183
Goals 23, 28, 29, 32, 44, 45,
79, 106, 107, 111-113, 117, 119,
125, 128, 151, 156, 168-175,
180, 184, 190, 197
Grievances: Fielding 13
Gripe session 133
Group vs Team 106
Growth 5, 52, 96, 118, 137,
147-148, 172, 187
Guide 18, 34, 35, 36, 128

H

Habits 33, 165, 178, 181,
187, 191
Hans Selye 185
Henry David Thoreau 165
Honesty 159
Horizontal communication 72
Human relations skills 21, 126
Human resources 94
Humor: Sense of 193
Humpty Dumpty 2, 23, 24, 27,
28, 30, 31, 32, 106, 121, 183

I

Impact 7, 51, 57, 66, 69, 74,
78-79, 80, 88, 105, 124, 125,
128, 131, 138, 148, 149, 151, 155,
168, 169-170, 172
Incentives 135
Increased productivity 75,
110, 146
Indira Gandhis 24
Informal communication 70, 72
Innovation 14, 43, 95
Innovative 46, 95

Inspire 3, 14, 18, 29, 30, 33,
38, 39, 125, 174
Integrity 27, 32, 34, 39,
42, 47, 126
Interact 69
Interdependence 113-114, 119
Interests 3, 90, 102, 110,
135-136, 160
Internal barrier 62-63, 79
Interruptions 67, 75, 80, 180
Interview 143-144, 147-149, 150-
155, 162, 163, 178

J

James M. Barrie 121
Japanese 124
Job-enrichment 62

K

Katherine Graham 167

L

Labor shortages 4
Lead by example 47
Leader:
        Become A 18;
        Business 9;
        On all levels 5;
        Develop as a 21;
        The word 24
Leadership Styles 25-26
Listen 36, 64, 65, 66, 75;

M

Major Galahad 25-26
Management 1-6, 9-11, 17-18,
20, 26, 28, 30, 43, 51, 56,
58-59, 64, 69, 70, 72, 85, 86,

89, 92, 97-98, 101,108, 113,
122-123, 125, 131, 132, 134,
135-136 , 146, 148, 150,
151, 165, 169, 184, 185,
Marion Hayes 105
Meditation 191
Middle management 5, 123
Miscommunication 59, 60, 68, 99
Morale 56, 90-91, 97, 110,
124, 126, 131, 136, 146,
153, 170, 172, 190
Motivated 87, 126, 129, 136, 138

N

New work ethic 11;
    Demands of 42
Non-leaders 26, 28-29, 38
Non-verbal messages 57, 78

O

Objectives:
    Accomplishing your
    company's 13;
    Achieving department's 29;
    Assignments and 21;
    Common 107;
    Company 2, 85;
    Deciding on 7;
    Accomplishing 56;
    Company & department 28;
    Office Olympics   115
Organize 13, 29, 56, 65,
74, 85, 114, 129;
    Getting: Staying 175

P

Participation 49, 92, 151
Peak performance 2, 3, 22, 50,
57, 79, 85, 88, 101, 111, 118,
127, 131, 134, 163
Perfectionist 195, 199
Performance 5, 7, 12-13, 18,
20, 22, 29, 30, 34, 36, 39,
76, 77, 92-93, 94, 96,
97, 100, 101, 145
Performance counseling 155-156,
159, 163
Performance evaluations 141
Personal goals 29, 111, 151, 170
Peter Block 42, 46
Policy 90, 143, 157;
    Open door policy 72
Poor communications 62
Power 2-3, 5, 8, 34,
42-46, 48, 50
Powerless employees   27
Praise 52, 77, 96, 97,
98, 135, 142, 150
Prejudices 64, 66, 79
Preoccupation 65, 80
Production staff 4
Productivity 4, 5, 20, 41, 46,
57, 59, 60, 65, 71, 75, 77,
85, 86-87, 90, 92, 93, 98,
101, 107-108, 110, 112,
118-119, 124-125, 126,
132-133, 143, 146,
150, 155, 161, 169, 170-171
Professional 5, 19, 108, 153,
165, 170;
    Balancing your life 184
Purpose 19, 28, 29, 45, 47, 53,
95, 147, 151, 154, 169, 172,
177, 179, 180;
    Finding that 170

Q

Quality:
Increasing 14

R

Records 20, 143, 145-146,
162, 197
Relationships
3, 21, 36, 79, 107-108, 110,
111, 116, 118, 144, 184, 185
Respect:
Demanding 12;
Earning the 5;
Losing employees 51;
Treating employees with 29;
Earning the 5
Responsibilities 20-21, 37, 43,
48, 83, 85, 86, 87, 89-90, 91,
93-94, 96, 100, 102, 128,
138, 169, 184, 192, 193, 195
Responsibility 2, 4, 8, 9-10,
11, 21, 27, 41, 42, 44, 46, 50,
56, 85, 87, 89-90, 93,
94, 96, 97, 99, 101-102,
106, 129, 135, 149, 154, 163,
184, 186, 193
Responsiveness 42
Result   3, 11, 16, 43, 47,
56, 59, 85, 86, 94, 127,
129, 139;
Behaviors and 20;
Bottom line 8;
Focus on 18;
Getting positive 29;
Poor 27;
Strategies that produce 6;
Top-notch 29
Rinke, Dr. Wolfe J. 108
Robert S. Bailey 23

Role 1, 7, 8, 9, 18, 21,
43, 46, 53, 56, 92, 94,
98, 102, 117, 121, 125, 128,
145, 149, 163, 169
Roles 8, 45, 47, 95, 106, 107,
108, 113, 118

S

Satisfaction:
Finding 167;
Increase job 119;
Needs-satisfaction 125;
Personal 5;
Primary reward 19;
Want 12
Selectivity 65, 79
Self-actualization 38
Self-development 22, 30, 38,
39, 101, 102
Self-Development Steps
39, 53, 81, 103, 119, 139, 164, 181
Self-esteem 91, 135
Skills 6, 13, 20-21, 24, 28-29,
36, 46-47, 49, 56, 63, 69,
74, 79, 80, 83, 84, 89, 90-91,
95, 106, 113-114, 126, 130,
145, 148, 153, 170-172
Strategy 73, 81, 88, 102,
118, 123, 139, 144, 146, 180, 188, 199
Stress 79, 183-194, 196-197
Sub-goals 113, 171
Subordinates 21, 28, 29, 48, 56-
57, 83-85, 134, 184
Supervision:
Basic 133;
Ineffective leader's 126
Survey of Employees 137
Suspension 158
Symbols 74, 116-117
Synergy 86, 101

T

Take notes 76
Task 2, 12, 13, 22, 24,
25, 30, 46, 69, 83, 86, 87
Teaching 96, 117, 130
Team 3, 6, 8, 9, 19, 20, 28,
29, 42, 44, 48, 50, 51, 57,
58-59, 65, 69, 76, 85, 88, 98,
99, 101, 103, 106-108,
110-113, 119, 134, 151, 160,
167, 190, 195,
>   Achieve team 106;
>   Building team 115;
>   Building a motivated team
>   126;
>   Building an effective team
>   108;
>   Commitment to the team 113;
>   Enabling your team 169, 184;
>   Goals 106;
>   Increasing output 172;
>   Morale 170;
>   Motivated 138;
>   Opportunities for 118;
>   People on your 116;
>   Reinforce the 117;
>   Successful 118;
>   Team spirit 110
>   Unity 117
Techniques 21, 30, 33, 38, 95,
118, 127, 133, 166, 189, 197
Theodore Friend III 31
Theodore Roosevelt 1
Theories 125, 150
Time management 165
Trial and error 37
Trust 27, 48, 50, 87, 106, 108,
111, 127, 153;

Betray 72;
Build 72;
Your instincts 46

U

Understanding Communication 57
United States 36, 124, 125, 138
Upper management 2, 10, 56,
64, 69, 70, 89, 97, 98, 113,
131, 135, 151, 169, 185
Upward communication 72

V

Vested power 3, 34
Vision: 31
>   Without 31;
>   Develop 10;
>   Go after 32;
>   Innovation and 14;
Visualize 21, 174

W

Warren Bennis 30-31
Work schedules:
>   Filling out 13